Praise for *Wet Behind the Ears*

"Every page rings true with the thrill of being an entrepreneur. It's an amazingly challenging life – but we entrepreneurs simply wouldn't have it any other way."

— DAVID PATCHELL-EVANS, CEO, GoodLife Fitness Clubs, and author of *Living the Good Life*

"What a wonderful book! Like its author, I also have a 'little rebel' inside and I wouldn't have succeeded in starting my own business without her. Inspirational!"

— KAREN VIVA-HAYNES, founder and owner of Viva Tastings Inc.

"A real eye-opener! Offers an 'I was there' perspective for those just getting started on the entrepreneurial path, those lost in the woods, and those who've made it through."

— ART HORN, CEO of HORN, a sales force development company, and author of *Gifts of Leadership* and *Face It*

Wet Behind the Ears

The Adventures of an Entrepreneur and the 7 Essential Lessons Learned

Bruno Gideon

mAtterhorn
PUBLISHING

Published in 2006 by
Matterhorn Publishing
20 Elm Avenue
Toronto, Ontario, Canada
M4W 1N3

Distributed by
Publishers Group Canada
9050 Shaugnessy Street
Vancouver, BC
V6P 6M9

Library and Archives Canada Cataloguing in Publication

Gideon, Bruno

Wet behind the ears : the adventures of an entrepreneur
and the seven essential lessons learned / Bruno Gideon.

ISBN 0-9732491-4-5

1. Gideon, Bruno.   2. Entrepreneurship.   3. Businessmen –
Canada – Biography.   4. Swiss Canadians – Biography.   I. Title.

HC112.5.G44A3 2006   338'.04'092   C2005-907081-1

Editorial: Donald G. Bastian, Bastian Publishing Services Ltd.
Design and typesetting: Daniel Crack, Kinetics Design
Author photograph by Joy von Tiedemann Photography Inc.

Printed and bound in Canada by Webcom

*In memory
of my parents,
Leo and Rosa Gideon*

You must learn from the mistakes of others.
You can't possibly live long enough
to make them all yourself.

– Sam Levenson

Contents

Foreword

THE concept of this book hit Bruno Gideon and me at precisely the same moment during a pleasant winter afternoon at a Toronto coffee shop. Not long before this, Bruno had published *Don't Take No for an Answer!* – the English edition of his German-language bestseller – and now we were discussing his next book. I was promoting the idea of a full-scale autobiography. It would tell the story of a man moving from childhood on a dairy farm in Switzerland to the heights of retail success in that country. The story of a man rising above anti-Semitic threats during World War II and emerging as one of his country's top business successes.

Bruno interrupted me mid-sermon. He would have nothing to do with such an effort, he said. He wanted to write a book that would help readers more directly. And that's when we had our light-bulb moment. He could tell his story vis-à-vis what stirred his passions most: the entrepreneurial life. He would write short and easy-to-read pieces focusing on the experiences of becoming, and being, an entrepreneur, drawing important lessons from those experiences for would-be or actual entrepreneurs.

"Readers will be able to determine whether they have the right stuff for being their own bosses," he said. "And if they do, they will benefit from seeing an entrepreneur in action."

Bruno added that he would tell his story warts and all, though he wasn't so sure his readers would learn from his mistakes. Entrepreneurs not only want to be their own bosses, he said, but they also want to make their own mistakes. He hoped, however, that his book would help them make more productive ones.

But Bruno wondered whether North American readers would want to read about the experiences of an entrepreneur in Switzerland. That question was quickly retired as we discussed the fact that entrepreneurs are entrepreneurs are entrepreneurs. It wouldn't matter if you plucked them off the streets of Nairobi, Naples, or Nice and plunked them down on the streets of Bombay, Berlin, or Brasilia – it wouldn't be long before they were developing new businesses.

And so I was privileged as his editor to see this book take shape. Bruno began writing about the influences of his childhood and early jobs that gave him the strong desire to become his own boss and the toughness to survive as an entrepreneur. He began putting onto paper the adventures and misadventures of working for Mövenpick and USEGO. He recounted the terror and exhilaration of becoming his own boss and starting the PickPay food discount chain and after that Switzerland's first computer store. He reflected on his "retirement" years, spent busily writing newspaper columns and books – and picking up stakes and starting life over again in a new country, Canada.

The result, I am very happy to say, is a book that celebrates the life of entrepreneurship as only one who was there could do. *Wet Behind the Ears* is an extraordinary tale full of energy and passion. Read it and reap!

– Donald G. Bastian
Toronto

Acknowledgments

FOR their assistance in writing and publishing this book, I must thank:

Dan Black, who supported me during the difficult and sometimes emotional process of writing.

My wife, Lucie, whose outstanding memory and love of detail prevented me from many oversights and mistakes.

Don Bastian, my editor, for his outstanding efforts on this project. His personal support and professional advice have been instrumental in making this book a reality.

– Bruno Gideon

Introduction

ENTREPRENEURSHIP is a popular topic these days. Open the business pages of any major newspaper and you're bound to find a column or at least some news stories on the topic. Business magazines include features on entrepreneurial issues. Larger bookstores have whole sections within their business sections devoted to books on or by entrepreneurs. This is a huge trend. Just consider how important the topic is to business schools, which offer courses on the subject. And ask your friends what their children want to do after they graduate. You'll be surprised by how many of them, no matter whether they are studying in the arts or the sciences, are looking to start their own businesses.

So why am I, through writing and publishing this book, contributing yet another discussion to the topic? Simply because what many of those venues for discussing entrepreneurship lack is a feel for the real – that is, a description of the nitty-gritty details of being an entrepreneur, written by "one who was there," with lessons for entrepreneurs drawn out of personal experiences.

That is exactly what *Wet Behind the Ears* is. It is a tour through my experiences of becoming and being an entrepreneur, complete with mistakes and successes and sorrows and joys. It is my hope that the book will help would-be entrepreneurs determine whether they have the right stuff for such a life, will provide practical advice for those who are already entrepreneurs, and will help everyone else understand the magnificent creatures who are called to this exciting life. The book clearly shows, sometimes to my own embarrassment, that we entrepreneurs are always a little wet behind the ears. We're always rushing into things we don't fully understand, taking risks, making mistakes. But ask any of us and we'll tell you we prefer living this way – it's much more exciting!

This book is not in any sense a textbook, even though it does teach the principles of entrepreneurship. It is a collection of stories from my life as an entrepreneur. Each story concludes with a section on what I learned from the experience. The book ends with a conclusion that lists the seven essential lessons of entrepreneurship. Although the facts of my case are mainly Swiss and go back many years, they are as universally valid as yesterday, anywhere, when it comes to the principles and experiences of running one's own business.

Please note that some of the names in the book have been changed to protect the innocent and the guilty.

In Part One, I recount the sometimes cruel experiences of growing up Jewish in "neutral" Switzerland during World War II. I show how what I call the little rebel inside me got me through some pretty tough times with the determination, and the thick skin, I would need to run my own business.

Part Two is about the making of an entrepreneur, but you will find that throughout the period covered, I was working "on the inside" – that is, for other people. These were not in any way wasted years, as I was, essentially, learning my trade on other people's tabs.

The heart of this book is Part Three, in which I tell the stories of my adventures as an entrepreneur. These were the years I dreamed of as I grew up and began working. The wonderful thing is that they turned out to be far, far better than even the wildest of my dreams.

Part Four is about my "retirement" years, but, as you will see, once you're an entrepreneur, you're always an entrepreneur, and life continues to be very busy and interesting indeed.

You are probably already sensing how passionate I am about being an entrepreneur. As you read on, you will see just why. You may even begin to feel the same way yourself.

Getting to Know the Rebel Within

Part One

Introduction

"**E**NTREPRENEURS** are born not made" is a common expression. I disagree. I don't believe that anyone is born an entrepreneur. People may from a very early age show personality traits that predispose them to being their own bosses, but what really shapes them are their experiences growing up, the influence of their parents and teachers, their schooling and summer job experiences, the advice of what I call their "little rebel," and sometimes sheer luck.

That certainly is true in my case, as the stories in this part will show. The little rebel inside me helped me believe in myself through some rather cruel experiences, and growing up as I did on a dairy farm, being sent away to a tough school for boys, and working as an intern for a negative boss molded me into the entrepreneur I would become.

Thank you,
little rebel

As is the case with most people, the experiences of my early years left a deep and lasting impression on me. However, most people did not have the fortune or misfortune I did of entering life during one of history's most dramatic periods. I was born in 1931 into a Jewish household of three brothers and one sister. Our parents, Leo and Rosa Gideon, owned a dairy farm outside Weinfelden, a village in eastern Switzerland just ten miles from the German border.

My eldest brother, Marcel, died one week after my birth. He was only thirteen, about to have his bar mitzvah. He had been stung on the lips by a bee the day I was born. Thus the first weeks and months of my young life were spent in a house draped in mourning – a dress rehearsal for my family of the grief we would feel over the killing of millions of innocent people, Jewish and others, by the Nazis.

In 1929, two years before I was born, the stock market had collapsed, setting off a chain of events that plunged the world into a depression. It was the beginning of the Dirty Thirties. Tragedy was in the air. Many people lost their jobs and all their money. Suicides were frequent. Poverty, anxiety, worry, and fear spread like wild-fire around the world.

Early in that decade, on January 30, 1933, a day that would prove to be the beginning of a brutal dictatorship, Hitler was sworn in as Chancellor of Germany.

My family, the only Jewish one in the region, was fully inte-grated into the life of our village. That was to change, however, once World War II began, in 1939. Most people continued to be decent to us, but some became Nazi lovers. The Nazi propaganda machine was stirring up feelings of anti-Semitism. Jews were being blamed for the hard times economically.

During the war, we heard rumors that the Nazis were systemat-ically killing civilians – most of them Jewish – in concentration camps. We thought it was a bad joke, but the rumors persisted. Meanwhile, Hitler's military were marching across, and flying over, Western and Eastern Europe. We did not know when he might invade Switzerland. We did know that if he did enter our country, our family would be murdered for the simple fact of being Jewish.

As a young boy growing up, I was not fully aware of the danger we were in. My parents and my siblings did not discuss the war when I was present. But it was impossible not to feel that we were close to being in real trouble. Disaster hung over us like the sword of Damocles.

Hatred against Jews was widespread – yes, even in "neutral" Switzerland. Friends of many years suddenly turned away from our family. Former classmates at grade school now avoided me; others attacked me physically over the smallest matters. Even some of the teachers became violent with me.

I had seen other children treated unfairly because of their dif-ferences: the girl with red hair; a boy who was cross-eyed; another student who didn't speak our local dialect. In those early years, I was unable to understand why children turned against their peers for such obviously unimportant traits. I did not know why I was being shunned by erstwhile friends. Even today, more than sixty years later, I am still unable to understand any form of discrimination and racism and their very existence continues to haunt me.

When I was in the sixth grade, my parents were summoned to a meeting with the principal of my public school in our small town. When they got home, they informed me that I could no longer attend the school. I was desolate. I didn't want to lose my friends. I hadn't done anything wrong. Why was I being singled out? Why did they want to get rid of me?

At the time and for several years following, I could not figure out what had happened. Schooling was compulsory, so throwing me out without a valid reason was illegal. I blamed the situation on myself. I was a difficult kid. The little rebel within me didn't make life easy for the people around me. I toyed with the idea that my parents were protecting me from the embarrassment of having to repeat a year because of poor performance. Still, deep down I knew that acting out, to use today's terminology, and being a slow learner were not legitimate grounds for such a decision.

The truth, of course, was that it was 1942, at the height of the Hitler mania. The Nazis had many supporters in our area and to be a Jewish boy – the only Jewish kid in the school – was not trendy, to say the least. There was nothing my parents could do but give in and send me elsewhere to continue my education. Maybe they were even a bit relieved that their difficult son would be out from under their feet for a while.

It was for a while, all right. They enrolled me in a five-year educational marathon at Kefikon, a renowned private boys' boarding school in a tiny village about ten miles from our farm. The name Kefikon has a hard-edged, penitentiary-like sound to it, and the place was indeed run very strictly. The school, founded in 1906, was located in a real nineteenth-century castle. It accommodated about sixty students. We ate and slept in-house and had to observe a rigid, to-the-minute schedule. If you were even just one minute late for something, you were punished.

The principal's name was Mr. Bach, an elderly gentleman,

probably in his early seventies, who was always elegantly dressed and carried an air of authority about him. We automatically felt inhibited around him, even before exchanging a word. We tried to avoid him as much as possible. If you were called to his office, you knew there was no escape. He would tell you to sit down and would continue working at his desk for several minutes without looking up. Finally, he would put his pen down, fix you with his steely blue eyes, and bring charges against you. Then it was time for sentencing. You might have to write, "I won't interrupt my teacher anymore" a hundred times or be ordered to go without dessert for a week. (The latter was a particularly harsh sentence considering the bland institutional food that preceded that course.) We were allowed to go home only once a month. A favorite punishment, therefore, was cancellation of this precious "go-home weekend." And of course that is exactly what happened to me on my first such weekend.

In my earliest days at Kefikon, I often stood at the very top of the tower of the castle, looking in the direction of my hometown, imagining my parents' farm, remembering my friends, thinking about our village and my old school. When I could no longer bear the loneliness, the tears would cascade down my cheeks.

Things came to a head in my second month at the school. On a Sunday morning, while the other boys were attending church, I snuck out and began walking in the direction of home. I walked for four hours, not bad for an eleven-year-old. As our farm came into sight, I was expecting a hero's welcome. I was looking forward to seeing my parents, my siblings, and my friends. I hoped that my description of life at Kefikon would mean never having to go back there again.

But when I walked into the kitchen, my father – who had probably been alerted to my escape – looked up from the table where he was reading a newspaper and said, "It is now two o'clock. Your train leaves in one hour and you are going to take it back to school."

No questions asked, no welcome given, no hugs, no support.

I never tried running away again. My existence at school might have been bleak, but my haven of safety had been closed to me. Where was I going to go?

Life at Kefikon really was like being in prison: you had no other option than to comply, and keeping out of trouble was the only way to make your life bearable. I learned how to stay one step ahead of the law, but at the same time I was determined to keep from being crushed. My little rebel helped me through many difficult times.

One teacher, a young man in his early thirties, was particularly cruel to me. He always ridiculed me in front of the whole class, which of course had the effect of turning everybody against me. Once he even beat me so hard that I fell out of the window. Fortunately we were on the first floor and I sustained only a few scrapes and bruises. Thanks to my little rebel, I had the temerity to complain to the principal, but my teacher flatly denied my accusations. No one, not even my parents, believed me.

Many years later, when I was well known as a journalist and author, I received a letter from this teacher. Here is what he wrote:

Dear Mr. Gideon:

I have received your address from the newspaper you write for. I used to call you Bruno, but that was a long, long time ago, when I was a young teacher at Kefikon. I am very old now, but I do remember that time very well. I was nasty and brutal to you and there is no way today to justify what I did. It has bothered me all my life and I can't stop thinking about how I hit you without a reason, how I ridiculed you in front of the class, and how I once even threw you out of a window.

I made your life very, very difficult and would like to apologize today for what I did. I was influenced by Hitler's propaganda and believed that all Jews were third-class people. Of course I know now that this is not true and I have many Jewish friends, but times then were different.

What I did to you bothers me beyond belief and I would like to apologize and ask for your forgiveness. I don't have a very long time to live and would like to have peace in my life. Please, Mr. Gideon, if you could forgive me, you would take a heavy burden off my heart.

I immediately called him and invited him to lunch. I met an old man, frail and in poor health, whom I didn't even recognize. I told him that his apology was accepted and explained how I had survived thanks to my little rebel. When we parted after lunch, he was at peace. I felt sorry that he had carried that burden with him for so long and grateful that I could relieve him of his pain. But I was also pleased to find that my mind had not played tricks on me – that my memories of this time were accurate.

Hitler killed himself on April 30, 1945, and the war in Europe ended over the following week. I was a teenager then, not even fourteen years old, with several more years to go before my personal war at Kefikon would be over. The truth of the human tragedy that Hitler instigated came to light slowly. His butchers had built concentration camps to kill millions of innocent civilians: men, women, children, and even newborn babies. Among the innocent: six million Jews. Hitler's victims had been absolutely powerless. They were totally at the mercy of their captors. My family's fear of this madman from the very beginning of the war and on had been quite rational.

I left Kefikon in 1948, just after turning seventeen, to begin training for a career in business. You have no idea what a relief it was to hear those big wooden doors of Kefikon close behind me for the last time.

What I learned
from this experience

1 We must treasure our little rebels.

I credit my little rebel for helping me survive, without significant scarring, the tremendous pressure put on me during my early years. Later I learned that many who succeed in business have just such a helper. I could back down or even cave in as needed, but I wasn't annihilated as long as my little rebel was with me. I came out of Kefikon hurt and depressed but unbroken. Once out from under that cruel regime, I was ready for a better future. More than that, I had the toughness and stamina it would take to succeed in business.

As I grew up, my little rebel stayed with me, although he did become more sophisticated in the way he said no.

Successful entrepreneurs come in all shapes and sizes. They are by no means of one personality type. I know introverted entrepreneurs and I know extroverted ones. I know aggressive entrepreneurs and I know quiet, steady-as-she-goes entrepreneurs. I know ones who have had a hard life and others who have sailed through without a care in the world. However, in my experience, by far the majority of entrepreneurs have a little rebel inside: a confidence that what they are doing is worthwhile and doable, a stubborn spirit in the face of unfair rules and regulations, and a determination to make things work, whatever the obstacles. If you have a little rebel inside you, let him help you.

2 To beware the power of publicity.

This may seem a strange conclusion to come to in the context of something so tragic as war and the killing of millions of innocent people, but several years after the war I began to realize the importance and danger of what I will call here "publicity." To this very day I am unable to comprehend why highly educated nations such as Germany and Austria, who gave the world geniuses like Mozart, Haydn, Bach, and many others, fell for the ignoble and dishonorable publicity tricks used by Hitler and his minions. But it underscored for me the power of publicity and advertising.

I don't want to say that Nazi propaganda was merely a form of publicity, but that is not completely off the mark. In every company that I built, in every consulting job I ever performed, and even in my daily thinking, I always emphasized the importance of publicity, or, to use today's expression, marketing. Marketing is the make-or-break factor of a company. But for marketing to work long-term, it has to be ethical. The Nazi madness acted as a powerful reminder to me of this critical fact.

3 Procrastination is never a good policy.

After what happened that fateful Sunday when my father sent me back to school, I withdrew from him. That was the wrong thing to do. I should have spoken out and explained what was happening at school and why I had run away, but at that time parents and teachers were undisputed authorities. Later, when I could challenge these authorities, I came to understand that he meant well and had a reason for what he did. At that point I should have talked to him and explained my remoteness. By then, however, it was too late; he had already died. This taught me, in business and in personal life, to face tough issues head on. Just as procrastination can be tragic in personal matters, so it can be destructive in business ones.

Three years
with Mr. Snappy

AT the end of my five-year sentence to Kefikon Boys' School, I found a job as a commercial apprentice in a food retail store called Coop, in Kreuzlingen, close to my home. Coop was one of Switzerland's largest food retail chains. At that time in our country, we had a three-year apprenticeship system for going into business. Apprentices would go to school for two or three afternoons a week and work for the company they were attached to the rest of the time. For a very low salary, they ran errands, helped out as needed, and learned some of the secrets of the trade. When I was an apprentice, I took English and French classes. I loved to write and won a school contest in story writing.

My boss's name was Bissig, which happens to be a German word meaning "snappy." The name could not have been more apt. My three years at Coop were not easy, mainly because of Mr. Snappy himself. He was less interested in teaching me the business than in using me as cheap labor. Mr. Snappy was unfriendly. He never offered compliments and was always brusque in his communication. We all tried to stay away from him to avoid his orders to do this or that, no questions asked. As far as I can remember, we never had any meetings with him in which our opinions were solicited or our efforts praised.

Although I was afraid of authorities and not very sure of myself, I had an inquisitive mind and learned a lot, thanks mostly to a long-term employee by the name of Olga. She was a chubby woman in her fifties. She had only one arm but I never dared ask her what happened because she was so natural in the way she wrote and talked and pointed things out. Olga was single and lived alone and always had time to help me at the office. In fact, she mentored me, as we would put it today, and was a welcome counterbalance to Mr. Snappy. But she was not only a nice, warm-hearted person, she was also an outspoken one.

One day during this time I called in sick but was really playing hookey from work and my classes. By coincidence, Olga met me on the street. She rebuffed me immediately.

"Learning is the most important goal for you and what you are doing is wrong," she said sternly but with some concern in her voice. "And lying about it doesn't make it any better."

I could take it from her because of the way she said it and because I knew she had my best interests at heart. Today I think of her as the first of many guardian angels that I have had the fortune to encounter.

Another gift from that apprenticeship was experiencing true friendship for the first time. A classmate, Rolf Zinke, became a close buddy whom I could trust and who trusted me. We studied together, went mountain climbing together, and spent our free time chasing girls together – well, not necessarily together. When our apprenticeship ended, in 1950, Rolf and I passed the final exams with exactly the same grade. We have remained close friends to this very day.

And so, with my commercial apprenticeship diploma clutched proudly in my hand and the uplifting words of the graduation ceremony reverberating in my ears, I was ready to conquer the world.

What I learned
from this experience

1 A "snappy" attitude hurts a company.

My three years as a commercial apprentice had little effect on me, but one thing of great worth came out of this time: witnessing how a boss's attitude can kill all initiative and enthusiasm. Some employees even destroyed merchandise in revenge for his negativism. He obviously didn't believe in the "co" in "co-workers" – or in "Coop," for that matter. Morale was very bad with all my colleagues either angry or terrified. None of us was even remotely tempted to do anything to help the company – not because we were lazy but because we weren't respected. I learned later that if you take your employees seriously and treat them with respect, they will act in the interests of your company. I found this to be true of everybody from those in the lowest positions right up to those in senior management.

2 The great value of people who speak their minds.

Olga brought me up short when she caught me not taking my education and work seriously. Her blend of sternness and concern was powerful. I made it a point from then on to welcome criticism from other people. For example, once I was in business for myself, I always told my assistants not to be afraid to speak up and challenge my policies and decisions and the way I treated employees and customers. This willingness to listen to negative feedback was the single most important principle in my career because it insured that I was not imprisoned by the views of naysayers or "yeasayers" but instead got my intelligence "from the street."

A test
of courage

AT the beginning of the 1950s, now that the major postwar reconstruction efforts were over, the economy was picking up in Switzerland and the rest of Europe. I was excited to be entering the real world at last.

Within days of beginning my job search, I found a job as a sales rep for a company that sold liquor to restaurants and bars. This company decided to take a chance on me even though I was only twenty years old and wasn't familiar with their trade. Of course, callow youth that I was, I was certain that I would be successful. Perhaps they were swayed by my confidence.

I was wrong, and so were they. To be honest, I was a total failure. Whatever the reason – whether I was too young to be credible as a liquor salesman or was intimidated by the forceful barmen or restaurant owners or was trying too hard because of my insecurity – I didn't make any sales at all. For a period of several months, I worked all day long, visited every possible customer in my region, and refused to give up, hiding my disappointment the best I could. (Fortunately, I didn't hit the booze that was so easily available to me.) My lack of sales weighed heavily on me and, with my salary being based on commissions, I was strapped financially.

And then I caught a break. The owner of a restaurant–bar that I was visiting in Zürich must have sensed my state of mind. He took one look at me, asked a few questions, and then out of the blue gave me a huge order. I was so shocked, I practically fell over myself with gratitude.

"Thank you very much for this order, sir," I said. "Thank you very much. I will personally supervise the order and make sure that it is filled correctly. Thank you, thank you . . ."

He just smiled and wished me luck.

My boss was pleased when I called him about my success. He complimented me and said, "Keep up the good work." However, his praise only made me feel more ill at ease. Nevertheless, I wanted to make sure that the order was filled correctly, so I went to the warehouse to supervise it personally.

Among other things, the order consisted of two cases of a high-priced, brand-name vermouth and three cases of a low-priced, no-brand vermouth. I couldn't believe my eyes when I saw that both vermouths had been bottled from the same barrel. The only difference, besides the price, was the label. I had to check into this, to keep my customer from being charged too much for the lower-quality merchandise. I tried to stop the warehouse employee in charge of the shipping.

"Wait a moment, there is a mistake," I said. "My customer ordered two qualities of vermouth and you are giving him the same one."

The man looked at me with surprise and said, "We always do it like this. No one has ever complained about it before." Then a roguish expression came over his face. "Why should we have two grades of vermouth if our clients are happy with one?" he said. "It is just a question of what is written on the label, and no one ever reads the label anyway."

I left the warehouse deeply disappointed in the ethical standards of my company. What bothered me most was the fact that the person who had given me my first break was being cheated. Did I tell him? Well, the title of this book isn't called *Wet Behind the Ears* for nothing. The answer is no. I simply did not have the courage to do so. Nor was I brave enough to confront the authorities in my company. But I couldn't stay there any longer. I quit my job. I never told my boss why I was leaving and he never asked.

The experience of being too young for this type of job showed me that I was not grown up enough to go into business for myself. I also realized that I had to do something to get clear of the shadows of my youth, though it would be more than a decade before I could deal with these problems once and for all.

What I learned
from this experience

1 To do my homework.

I made the mistake of accepting the first job offer that came along. A little research and thought would have revealed to me that I was too young for the job and lacked the appropriate qualifications. Of course, my little rebel was right in there praising me for having found a job within days while the others from my program were still searching. But just as I lacked courage in talking to my duped customer or my conniving bosses, so I lacked the courage to say no to the first paying job that I bumped into. In this case, I was young and didn't lose much time, but similar situations happened to me later in my life where doing my homework would have saved me a lot of time and money.

2 The importance of giving people a leg up.

The person who gave me that big order did me an enormous favor, boosting my self-confidence in the process. He may have thought little of it, but he helped a young person trying to find his sea legs and did so with few words and no expectation of a reward. Small gesture though it may have been, it was very important to me at the time. Today, many years later, I try to do the same thing for others. Selling can be a lonely business, with twenty rejections for every yes. It's true that salespeople have to grow a thick skin, but even the toughest among them is helped by the occasional helpful gesture. And this is true not just of salespeople. Helping people has become one of my highest priorities.

No, I don't
eat spinach!

ONE night a few years ago, living in Toronto and retired from active business, I had a chilling dream that told me I had to visit my parents' grave. As my parents had passed away many years before that – my father in 1948 at the age of sixty-seven and my mother in 1972 at the age of seventy-seven – they rarely came to my mind. I didn't pay much attention to the dream.

I was living my life – a happy life – in a new country and for the most part had forgotten the hard times of my early years. But the dream became a recurring one and finally I gave in and made the decision to visit my parents' gravesite the next time I was in Switzerland. Once that decision was made, the dreams stopped.

It was a gray Sunday afternoon in the fall when I walked up to my parents' burial place in the Jewish cemetery in Zürich. It is a Jewish custom for visitors to put a little stone on the tombstone, and I was surprised to see, by the number of stones on my parents' tombstone, that many people had visited recently, so many years after their passing.

I sat down and was trying to imagine my mother and father's faces when a deep depression came over me. I felt very uncomfortable and wanted to leave but couldn't. A terrifying memory gripped me.

I was about ten years old, the youngest of four siblings. Like any card-carrying youngster, I detested spinach and absolutely refused to eat it. I would eat everything else on my plate but wouldn't touch the green glop staring up at me. Adopting this policy in our family took a lot of courage or sheer orneriness. The rule was that every plate had to be finished. Whoever failed to comply was in for punishment, such as not being allowed to get up from the dinner table until the offending food was eaten, standing in a corner for an eternity, or being dispatched to bed hours before bedtime. My father was the police force, prosecution, judge, and jury. His will was the law.

One day when I once again refused to eat spinach, my father pinched my nose and when I opened my mouth to breathe he stuffed the spinach into my mouth. Despite having achieved his objective, he still sent me to bed early. When I woke up the next morning, the spinach was still in the corner of my mouth. Unfortunately, I was caught when I spit it out.

Such behavior had consequences. The following Sunday, my parents locked me in an empty room with nothing to eat but a plate of spinach. They promised that I would be freed when the plate was empty. A short time later I shouted through the closed door that the plate was empty.

My mother opened the door. Without saying a word, I swept past the assembled family, grabbed some books and toys, and quietly went into the kitchen, locking and bolting the door. I was prepared to stay there forever.

In spite of my father's threats, my mother's urgent requests, and my brothers' and sister's appeals, I refused to open the door. Then I heard a noise outside the window. My elder brother had been deployed to try to get into the kitchen with a ladder. I closed the shutter tight and barricaded it. For once I had the upper hand and felt safe.

Eventually our dog Bless was heard scraping the floor in the room where I had just been incarcerated, and my parents found the spinach that I had hidden under the carpet. More threats battered the kitchen door. They were going to break the door down, they said. They were going to get the police, then I'd be sorry. I didn't budge.

Hours passed and it got dark. There wasn't much courage left in my young heart. I was lonely and afraid of the power of my "enemies" and the punishment that surely awaited me. After a long period of silence, my mother came to the door. She begged me to open it, promising that nothing would happen to me if I complied. That was a great relief, but experience with my father prompted me to say, in a tiny voice, "I'll open the door if Father comes to the door and promises not to punish me."

About five minutes later my father came to the door and said, "Bruno, you can come out – nothing is going to happen to you."

I opened the door, elated that my ordeal was over and that I had won. But without a word, my father grabbed me by my ears, dragged me to his bedroom, told me to lower my pants, took a broom that he had been placed there for just this task, and hit my buttocks so hard that I could not sit down for days.

The pain eventually subsided, but for years to come I could not forgive my father for deceiving me, and so brutally. This was the incident that finally broke me and turned me into a frightened boy with low self-esteem. I became reclusive. It took me many years to fully recover.

Now, as darkness fell over the cemetery, I thought of my parents and my life. I was grateful that I had been able to succeed in spite of the drawbacks of my early years. That I was a balanced person in spite of all the bad experiences that had been stuffed into my emotional knapsack. (See the story "Life on the Couch" later in this book.) I left the cemetery deep in thought, promising to return.

When I did, shortly afterward, I "talked" to my parents at length. This silent and very emotional dialogue helped me understand why my father reacted the way he did. Times were tough. His anxiety was easily spiked by the slightest waste of our scarce resources. Furthermore, he was completely in step with what he understood to be his role as a father and with the educational practices of the time. And the little stones on the tombstone also told the story that others respected and loved them.

More positive memories of him came back to me. Shortly after the war, the Red Cross asked him to accommodate four Jewish boys from Vienna who had survived the war because they had been hidden. The youngest, Josef, was ten years old. The others – Otto, Eric, and Egon – were a few years older. When they came to stay with us they were very frightened. However, the time they spent with us on our farm and in our village was beneficial to them. When they left, they were ready to get on with their lives. I am still in contact with Josef, who lives in Vienna, but have lost contact with the others.

I was surprised, and gratified, to receive this e-mail just as this book was about to go to press:

Dear Bruno Gideon,

I am the sister of Hans M. and grew up in Weinfelden.
I am a few years younger than you are. I vividly remember those times and will never forget what Pastor Sieber told us in our religious-education classes: that the only people in our village exhibiting Christian charity was the Jewish family, the Gideons. We knew that your family had many refugees living in your home during the war and saved the lives of many.
I will never forget those times, and his words still ring in my ears today.

Verena M.

My youthful trials and tribulations had caused these memories to be repressed, too, even though they showed the good side of my father and family.

Suddenly, with tears flowing down my cheeks, I was able to accept reality, to let go and focus on the present. It was there, in the cemetery, that I began to understand what I couldn't comprehend when I was a boy. My father was by far not the brutal person I remembered. There was another side to the story.

"Rest in peace," I said to him and my mother. With that, I was finally able to be at peace with myself.

What I learned from this experience

1 The importance of letting go.

"Letting go" is an overused phrase, but there is a lot of truth to it. In fact, I would revise "the importance of letting go" to "the necessity of letting go." When I faced the horrible memory of that injustice perpetrated on a preteen boy, and when I forgave my parents – mainly by coming to understand that their motives were not evil – I became free emotionally. I only wish I had gone through this experience earlier in my life.

It is surprising how many entrepreneurs carry hurts and injustices around, neutering their ability to deal openly with suppliers, customers, and employees. Out of their experiences of hurt, they hold themselves back from people. This doesn't mean they won't be successful. Many will, but they will pay a stiff price emotionally and physically. Letting go would make their life easier and much more enjoyable.

2 It takes one to know one.

Even before experiencing this release, and even before reaching this level of self-knowledge, I was often able to detect a forceful spirit in people – the kind of people who might well have done what I did when I was confronted by spinach on my plate. We were like a secret brotherhood or sisterhood.

I always thought twice before hiring people with a little rebel inside them, because to do so was a gamble. I had experienced difficulties with overly determined types and knew there was a fine line between determination and stubbornness. They often challenged my authority or the authority of company policies, even on issues that should have been routine. What I learned to look for was people who not only had strength of mind but also showed flexibility of character. When I found people with those two characteristics, I found myself some great workers. Inevitably, they moved up the ranks quickly, and many of them went on to start businesses of their own.

Dairy farmer, entrepreneur

THOUGH perhaps not in today's sense of the term, my father was an entrepreneur. I learned many valuable lessons from him that helped me in business. You could say of my move from his farm to the business world that you can take the entrepreneur off the farm, but you can't take the farm off the entrepreneur.

Accompanied by our farm laborer, my father often sold cattle to farmers in the area at the regular cattle markets held in other parts of Switzerland.

The negotiation and sales process at these markets was unique. The buyer walked around the cow and touched it here and there, evaluating the thickness of the skin, the soundness of the bones, and the condition of the teeth. If at all interested, he asked for the price. My father told him a price and the buyer made a counter-offer. The two looked at each other, trying to assess each other's limits, and then the bargaining would begin in earnest.

Both parties would hold their right hands out palm side up. Each price mentioned in the bartering would elicit a friendly slap to the other's hand. Once they had reached a price that was acceptable to both of them, the slap was replaced with a handshake, which concluded the agreement between the parties. There was no paperwork, no written agreement. My father simply penciled the name of the buyer and the price in a little black book that he always carried with him, and that was it.

These verbal agreements were as good as a written contract. No one ever failed to live up to their commitment. That wouldn't have played well in such a close-knit community. If the farmer was not able to pay the whole amount, he was given extra time, but even then nothing was put into writing. How different from today's business world, where teams of lawyers circle overhead, ready to parachute down to produce reams of paperwork when deals are made.

My father and his peers thought of themselves as farmers, not entrepreneurs. But entrepreneurs they were. Most of them owned their own farms or were still paying the bank for them. They had to work with bankers and be alert to changes in the market, whether caused by weather patterns or supply issues. They opened their "shops" every morning and closed them every night. They had to manage their inventory of tools, buy the number of cattle that they could sell, and put money aside for a rainy day. And they had to work very hard day after day, just like any real entrepreneur.

For the longest time, because of my own troubles with my father and my desire to get off the farm, I did not realize how much being the son of a dairy farmer had prepared me for business. Many years later, I saw more clearly that my father's success was in fact the result of his own keen business sense. Running a farm took independence of mind, a determination to succeed, and razor-sharp judgment about what adjustments to make in the farmer's constant dance with the elements and market trends.

One day one of our cows was sick and couldn't stand up. She was diagnosed with foot-and-mouth disease, which was an absolute disaster for our farm. This disease is a highly contagious viral illness that affects cloven-hoofed animals such as cattle, sheep, and pigs. It causes sores, blisters, and fever and is deadly for the livestock but harmless to people. The police ordered us to kill all our cows and calves, which of course was agonizing to all of us – they were not just farm animals; we had an emotional attachment to them.

The police immediately put up roadblocks and disinfection barriers around our property. No one was allowed to visit us for several weeks, nor were we allowed to leave the farm. Food was ordered by telephone and brought to the fence, where we could pick it up only after the delivery person had left.

My father was totally unprepared for this disaster. Not only did it disrupt our daily routine, such as milking the cows, taking milk to the collecting points, and all the other tasks that are important on a farm, it also changed our daily life. I could not go to school and we had no social contact with anybody outside. It was also disastrous financially, even though part of the damage would be covered by insurance later.

While my father wasn't prepared for this event, he did respond to it quickly and decisively. Immediately after the ban was declared, he picked up the phone and began negotiating the purchase of new animals. He never complained about our bad luck but focused entirely on what was going to happen once the crisis had passed. The day after the ban was lifted, new animals were delivered to the farm and life went on as normal.

What I learned
from this experience

1 Honesty is the best policy – and saves on lawyers' fees.

I shudder to think of the amount of money I spent on lawyers during my career. I appreciated their skills. I knew I needed them on my side. I consulted them many times when threatened with court cases or brought up short by municipal or national laws. But in many ways they were a necessary evil. Slaps on the hand followed by a handshake would have made my business, and that of others, much more efficient and profitable. Unfortunately, in today's business world we just can't trust that everyone will be as honest as those good Swiss farmers.

2 The importance of breeding.

There's something to be said for "breeding," not just with cattle but with people. Several times in my experience, children of great entrepreneurs or business leaders had to step in and run the family business because of unforeseen circumstances. Workers in these businesses would roll their eyes at the prospects of these neophytes taking over. Many of the latter, after all, were parachuted in from their arts courses or their ceaseless round of parties, courtesy of Daddy's money. But very often these kids proved to be a success, due to something they must have picked up by growing up "around the shop." It didn't matter whether their parents were farmers, teachers, lawyers, shopkeepers, civil servants, or politicians, certain helpful characteristics rubbed off.

When I was looking for employees, I always asked a lot of questions in order to find out as much as I could about their growing-up years. I often found clues in their answers that helped me hire the right people for the right jobs.

3 The importance of ownership.

Financial planners are fond of saying that the best way to prosper is to own something, even if only through the purchase of a company's shares. For me, ownership meant so much more – even more than profits. I was happiest when I was my own boss. I would have rather made less money as my own boss than more working for someone else.

When hiring workers for very specific roles, I knew to avoid signing up people with this ownership drive. But when hiring management, I looked for precisely such people. I knew that I would lose some of them to their own businesses, but I knew I would gain something from their entrepreneurial drive the way.

The Making of an Entrepreneur

Part Two

Introduction

WHEN it comes to being an entrepreneur, the devil is in the details. You don't start your own business by sitting around elegantly thinking big thoughts and dreaming big dreams. No, as in my own case, for example, you do it by being a busboy and a pot scrubber and by sucking everything of value out of your experiences working for other people and companies.

Two other phrases describe this process, as well: "you make your own breaks" and "you have to be good to be lucky." Entrepreneurs make their opportunities and watch for their opportunities and grab their opportunities and get the most they possibly can from their opportunities.

In this part of the book I am not yet that person I always dreamed of being. I am still "working for the man." I still face some issues of self-confidence. But I know now that I was was getting close to the wonderful life I was about to live. Very close, indeed.

A busboy
in Rome

WHEN my father passed away, he left my brothers, sister, and me some money. My portion was placed in a trust until my twentieth birthday, the full legal age in Switzerland. I decided to use this money for my education; I wanted to learn languages and study the hotel business.

The idea of hotel work didn't spring out of nowhere. It was prompted partly by a family situation.

One evening, when I was still a teen, my father, who never consulted anyone when he made decisions, announced to my mother while we were having dinner, "I bought a property in our village today, a hotel with a restaurant. Starting tomorrow, you will work there and manage it."

My mother, usually very compliant, was vehemently opposed to this directive. I can still remember her response.

"No," she said very firmly, "I am not in the hotel business and I am not going to work there – absolutely not. Over my dead body!"

Whereupon she and my father withdrew to their bedroom. I don't know what happened there, but the next morning, without a word, out the door she went to manage the hotel. It was located in the center of the little town near where we lived, and it became an important gathering place not only for our family and the people of the village but also for people escaping the brutal war raging in Germany.

It was customary in our rural area for the owner of the local hotel to greet every guest by name and with a handshake, and you'd better not make any mistakes. My mother was very good at remembering names. That ability, combined with her equally strong gift of making people feel at ease, helped make our little establishment very popular. Seeing my mother happy in her job, especially considering how opposed to it she was at the beginning, made me think about entering the same business. I always felt at ease in this environment. I liked the contact with new and returning customers, the opportunity to deal with people of all types, and the challenge of making their stay as pleasant as possible.

The best place to study the hotel business and learn every angle of the trade was in the French-speaking part of Switzerland at the prestigious Ecole hôtelière de Lausanne, or Hotel Trade School of Lausanne. I applied and was accepted.

The hotel school was a very large establishment with several buildings on the campus. There were several hundred students attending from more than twelve different countries. Classes were given in French and English.

When I began my schooling there, on a warm June afternoon, I had stars in my eyes about swanning around posh hotels in elegant attire, the very soul of grace and courtliness. But as always in life, there was a gap between the dreams and the reality, and in this case the gap was very wide. I didn't realize how tough life in the hotel business would be. But it also was an invaluable learning experience. Without a doubt this phase of my life set the stage for my future success in running my own businesses.

The hotel school in Lausanne is the foremost educational institute in Europe for the international hospitality industry. I was delighted to have been accepted into its program. The school was attended at that time by many famous names, such as Nick (Nicky) Hilton of the Hilton dynasty, a extremely handsome young man. We didn't see him very much, not only because he preferred to live at the fashionable Palace Hotel in Lausanne instead of the school dormitory, but also because of his romantic liaison with Liz Taylor. The Hilton hotel chain sponsored a prize for best student of the year but Nick never had a chance of winning. His attendance was spotty and he left the school prematurely, not entirely of his own choosing.

Why was – and is – the school so successful? Because of the exceptional way it teaches its students. It focuses on the theoretical side of hospitality in classes during the day, following that up with internship training for several months in a hotel anywhere in Europe, at the choice of the school.

The curriculum was divided into four departments – service, kitchen, front desk, and administration – and was cleverly organized. Classes lasted all day, except for periods of practical work. For example, the kitchen students cooked the meals, and the service students served them to their classmates. I decided to begin with the service department. After four months of mostly academic work, I was sent to be a waiter at the Hotel Quirinale in Rome, at that time the number-one hotel in the Eternal City.

I had more than a few butterflies over the prospect of working in a city so far away where I wouldn't be able to speak the language – I had whole colonies of them. Once I got to Rome, I was even more aware that I was a complete stranger in a city where everything was different: the work, the culture, and the language. My uneasiness grew when I saw the hotel, an impressive and intimidating building in the center of the city. It was certainly a very high-end place. Limousines were lined up out front, butlers and chauffeurs were dashing about everywhere, and there was even an entrance from the hotel right into the Rome Opera

House. This was going to be my home for the next five or six months?

I was looking forward to an interview with the maître d', my future boss, who would be welcoming me to his team of waiters. Monsieur Albert, an elderly and very elegant gentleman of French origin, greeted me with a handshake and spoke to me in elegant Italian.

"Benvenuti a Roma!" he said. "Lo sapevate che diamo un servizio eccellente a tutti i nostri clienti? Avete qualche domanda . . ."

My slack-jawed expression must have tipped him off that I had no idea what was he talking about. He switched to French and said that, because of my lack of Italian, I wasn't qualified to be a waiter and would have to work as a busboy. What a shock! I tried to protest, knowing full well that he was appointing me to the lowest level in the hierarchy of a service team.

"Busboy?" I said to him in French. "But I speak French and German and English and learned to be a waiter at the hotel school in Lausanne and they sent me here to be a waiter . . ."

Monsieur Albert waved me away like a pesky fly. "Learn to speak Italian and let me know when you can make conversation and I'll see what I can do," he said. "You will start tomorrow."

And so my first real job in the hotel business was as one of five busboys whose responsibility was nothing more than to clean the tables and reset them with fresh tablecloths, dishes, cutlery, and napkins.

But of course he was right. How could I have hoped to be a waiter in Italy without speaking Italian? A waiter who doesn't speak the language of the guests at table is worthless. How stupid of me. But I could still correct my situation. I decided to take classes in Italian right away and learn the language as quickly as I could.

We five busboys – all of us teenagers – slept in the same room high up on the top floor of the hotel, right under the roof. There was just one bathroom for all of us, no air conditioning, and just one small window on the world, overlooking the yard at the back of the hotel. It was unbearably hot up there. I was learning about summers in Rome the hard way.

The job, which began the next day, was easy. There wasn't much to learn. The one thing we would come to detest about our work was the food. Being at the lowest level of the service team, we ate alone. Our lunches and dinners were typical Italian fare: spaghetti. We had spaghetti for lunch and spaghetti for dinner, spaghetti on Monday and every other day of the week, and that was it. Well, not exactly. There was one exception: once a year they gave the busboys some meat: the Christmas dinner was chicken – with spaghetti, of course.

What is a proper busboy to do in such a situation? Simple: take food from where there was plenty – the customers' tables. The way the five us contrived to do this was ingenious and a great example of teamwork. While fruit baskets were still on the table, some of us fruit-napped by putting some of the baskets' yieldings into napkins. The napkins in turn went into the laundry bags which were regularly transferred to the back of the kitchen, where we would seize upon and devour the food at our earliest opportunity. We did the same with bread, dessert, and anything else we could scrounge up.

We virtually unionized our activities. There was the napping team and the cleaning team. The former relieved tables of their bounty and the latter carefully retrieved the bounty from the laundry bags. We ran our gambit under a strict code of ethics. The treasures were distributed equally. Honor among thieves, you might say. No one ever discovered our little game.

The other busboys were about my age but lacked an education. They came from simple backgrounds in rural Italy. Nevertheless, they accepted me unconditionally from the very beginning, even though they were dealing with a foreigner who at first spoke almost no Italian. It was in this hotel, while working at the bottom of the hotel hierarchy, that I experienced what open-mindedness and true tolerance meant. I felt very much accepted.

I recall one rather embarrassing incident. One day, when collecting the plates from the tables, my little rebel kicked in and told me that I could collect far more plates than the other busboys. With a matter-of-fact expression on my face, I loaded one plate after another until I finally held a huge stack between my hands, about thirty plates or so. Without looking right or left, but knowing that the diners were watching me, I walked proudly toward the kitchen. I still don't know how it happened – perhaps I stumbled over a bump on the floor or maybe one of the customers tripped me under the table – but suddenly I lost my balance and in extreme slow-motion at first but then faster and faster and with a terrible noise, all the plates and I fell on the floor.

I wasn't hurt and got up immediately, and everybody came running to help me clean up the mess. The clients at the tables didn't seem to be too disturbed – but a small group near the place where I fell couldn't stop laughing. It had taken only a split second for the proud busboy to be transformed into a humiliated young man.

The incident didn't have any repercussions for me. I didn't even have to pay for the destroyed plates. But I knew that my little rebel, who had helped me so many times, had tricked me this time.

After five months of regular Italian lessons, I asked for another meeting with Monsieur Albert. In the best Italian that I could muster – I had rehearsed my lines – I told him, "Thank you, Monsieur Albert, for having given me the experience of working in your hotel for five months."

He answered with surprise in his voice, "I remember now – hotel school in Lausanne, right? But you came here without speaking Italian and now you have a Roman dialect! How come . . ."

I told him that I had taken lessons and learned the dialect from my colleagues. And then he paid me a nice compliment by offering me a job as a waiter. I thanked him but kindly declined because I had to go back to hotel school for the next course.

However, I needed a certificate as a waiter, not as a busboy, for my final diploma. We agreed that I would work for one week as a waiter and they would give me the certificate, which is exactly what happened.

What I learned
from this experience

1 Tolerance works.

It wasn't the glories of the hotel and Rome that made the strongest impression on me. No, it was my busboy colleagues. The five of us never focused on our differences but on our work as a team. This was a new experience for me. Courtesy of my five long years at Kefikon, I assumed that I would experience anti-Semitism, unfairness, and hatred at their hands. What a gift to see that not everyone was this way. This experience was an example of tolerance that I always try to practice myself.

2 There is always a way out.

When I arrived in Rome and was demoted to being a busboy, I didn't give up. I saw that learning Italian was the way out, and being offered the job of waiter at the end of my stay proved me right. Successful entrepreneurs do not balk at obstacles – and what is the life of entrepreneurship but a series of obstacles? No, they immediately look for a way around them. There is always a way, however tempting it may be to resign oneself to failure out of disappointment, frustration, or loneliness.

3 Life is more than work.

My stay in Rome gave me a bonus that I will always treasure: the unbelievable culture of a truly great city. To come to such a city at such a young age, completely unprepared for what it had to offer, made a big impression on me. We had plenty of free time and I regularly visited the Vatican Museum, which houses the largest art collection in the world; the magnificent St. Peter's Basilica, the largest church in the world; the Sistine Chapel with its marvelous ceiling paintings by Michelangelo; the statue of Moses in San

Pietro in Vincoli; and many other breathtakingly beautiful places. I believe that everything in life happens for a reason. If there's such a thing as good culture shock, that's what I experienced in Rome. And while there, I tossed a coin in the Trevi Fountain – a way to ensure that I would return to Rome, which I did whenever I could.

Smelling eggs
in Lausanne

BACK in Lausanne, I was ready to take the hotel school's second program, training in cooking. The school had a full-blown professional kitchen, in which we cooked three meals a day for the students in the other classes and for the school's teachers and administrators.

A six-month course was not long enough, of course, to make a real executive chef out of me, but it was enough to give me a feel for how a kitchen is run. Our chef was nice but very strict and controlling. I believe that he had to be authoritarian – it wasn't easy to take a bunch of young people and train them to work together. Still, it was fun to cook all day long.

I worked in different departments. I peeled and chopped vegetables, prepared demi-glace, cut meat, kneaded dough, beat egg whites, and whipped cream. The battered egg whites had to be so thick that when the copper bowl was turned upside down, they wouldn't fall out. We had to make sure the job was well done, because the chef would sometimes test our work by holding it over our heads.

I vividly remember one incident early in my training. We were taught an interesting routine for breaking eggs. In one motion and with one hand, we grabbed an egg, broke it against a sharp object, smelled it, and then emptied it into the pot and discarded the eggshell. Our chef told us that we always had to smell the eggs so that a rotten one could be thrown away before it could do any damage.

One day I had to break 120 eggs into a pot – if I remember correctly, crêpes were on the menu. As expected, I followed the protocol that we had been taught. But the job was taking too long and I was getting bored. My little rebel kicked in and whispered, "Why don't you show them how fast you can be? You don't have to smell every egg. Go for it and speed it up! They will all envy you your pace."

My little rebel was right: it was fun to break one egg after another, putting them directly into the pot. Soon I was racing against myself, trying to crack one more egg per minute. I was calculating how long it would take to crack the remaining eggs, when it happened: a foul smell filled the kitchen, a smell so terrible that everyone around me reared back sniffing, looking at each other and wondering, "Who cut the cheese?"

Then came the furious voice behind me, "Did you smell every single egg before putting them into the pot, as you were told?"

It was the chef.

"Well, yes, I mean – the first ones were all okay, and then . . ." I answered.

I didn't have to finish the sentence. While everyone stared at me, he threw the contents of the pot, and my hopes for glory, down the drain.

I had to do the whole thing all over again. When the little rebel tried his number on me again, I sent him packing – one such embarrassment was enough. I eventually had to pay out of my own pocket for eighty-four eggs.

Before long it was time to move on to the next step: apprenticeship in a first-class hotel kitchen. The school sent me to

France, to the Hotel des Bains et de la Plage in Pornichet, a small village right on the Atlantic Ocean. The hotel had a beautiful view of the ocean and I enjoyed every minute of my time there. I loved the work and the environment and my colleagues and the chef. The work was so enjoyable I didn't consider it to be work at all but just another form of vacationing. And we had a lot of free time to swim in the ocean and hang out in the village.

The chef's name was Monsieur Viale, a very friendly and communicative middle-aged professional who treated his employees with respect, never raising his voice. Everybody loved him. His approach to training and managing us helped us form into a real team without any tension between departments. I witnessed several incidents when someone made a mistake or, out of carelessness, destroyed some food. He always took the incident seriously but never vented his wrath on the perpetrator. Instead, he focused on repairing the damage.

As was the case at the hotel in Rome, the kitchen was organized into a strict hierarchy. Different departments were responsible for specific parts of the meal. There was the *entremetier*, who was responsible for all vegetables, fries, and other potato and rice dishes. There was the *saucier*, responsible for all the meat and gravy with the exception of the meat that the *garde manger* prepared. This last person was responsible for deboning huge pieces of meat as he cut them down to portion sizes. His main responsibility, however, was the cold cuisine, mainly salads. Then there was the *poissonier*, who did everything related to fish and – our specialty – lobster. And I shouldn't forget the *patissier*, the pastry chef who created all the desserts. Finally there was the *casserolier*, the pot scrubber, who cleaned all the baking trays, the frying pans, and the heavy-duty copper pots.

One day, Monsieur Viale assembled the entire kitchen staff and informed us that the pot scrubber was going to be away for two weeks. He asked who would volunteer to do the job during his absence.

I raised my hand and said, "I'll do it."

Monsieur Viale looked at me with astonishment and said, "Are you sure you are up to it, Bruno? It is pretty hard work."

He had always been nice to me and I wanted to be nice to him. So I said, with a flourish, "No problem! I can do it and I'll be happy to help you out."

And thus, as there were no other takers, I became the pot scrubber for two weeks.

I had no idea of what I was getting myself into. A pot scrubber is a pot scrubber is a pot scrubber, is what I thought. Obviously my talent for observation was not highly developed then. I began my new responsibilities the next morning and immediately understood the surprise over my decision. Carrying the huge and heavy copper pots around all by myself and cleaning them thoroughly was like eight hours of uninterrupted fitness training. Sometimes the pots were burned and required even more elbow grease.

As I scrubbed away, I realized that my colleagues were watching for me to give up. I later learned that they had made bets on how long I would last. But I was determined to finish the two weeks of slave labor no matter what. And I did.

Two positive things came out of this experience. The first was how well I slept after my daily ordeal. Each day, as soon as my work was done, I went to bed and sank into a luxurious and lengthy state of unconsciousness.

The second almost made me cry. When the two weeks were over and the real pot scrubber replaced me, everybody in the kitchen applauded me.

I left the Hotel des Bains et de la Plage in September, when summer was almost over. I had learned a lot there, not only about cooking, but also about how to manage people. Monsieur Viale was a shining role model for me.

What I learned
from this experience

1 The art of breaking eggs.

Always smell an egg before putting it into the pan!

2 What real authority is all about.

Monsieur Viale taught me by example that a boss does not have to assert his authority by behaving like a sergeant in a boot camp. He never raised his voice. He trusted his co-workers from the very start and showed them that trust in many ways. I learned later that when my colleagues were betting on how long I would last as a pot scrubber, Monsieur Viale bet in my favor. I wasn't surprised. He understood that teamwork is the highest goal of any group working together, and he achieved it through commiting himself to the team. I only worked for him for six months, but I'll never forget him.

3 Every job is important and necessary.

A five-star kitchen is dependent not just on a fabulous chef and up-and-coming sous chefs but also on a good pot scrubber. The same thing is true in any job or professional endeavor. It is vitally important that every level within a company works well. Low-level jobs – if there even are such things – are very important.

Picked by Mövenpick

IT was an extremely busy day at the front desk. Switching between German, French, English, and Italian, I was dealing with a cascade of requests from guests. Meanwhile, I kept noticing a gentleman opposite me, who just stood there, observing me. I didn't know who this man was, but I certainly knew this about him: if he was trying to make me feel uncomfortable, he was succeeding.

I was in my mid-twenties, enjoying my job as a front desk clerk at the Hotel Elite, a five-star hotel in the center of Zürich. I derived a lot of pleasure from communicating with our guests as I assisted them with their wishes and made them feel at home.

There was a downside to the job, however, and that was the very long hours with almost no time for a private life. I had just begun dating a young woman, Lucie, whom I liked very much. We would have loved having more time to ourselves. I toyed with the idea of changing my job, but jobs at that time were difficult to find. Besides, I knew that I wasn't made for quiet, predictable work in an office. I needed contact with the public, a need that my current position filled very well.

To my irritation, the gentleman just kept standing there taking in my every word and action. Finally, in a rare moment when there were no guests to attend to, I decided to ask him if I could be of any service. But before I could say anything, he came toward me and introduced himself. He was none other than Ueli Prager, the well-known founder and owner of a new restaurant chain called Mövenpick. To my surprise – shock, really – he offered me a position as a buyer in Mövenpick's head office. A miracle! No résumé, no interview, no references, yet just like that, a new and apparently interesting job!

I accepted on the spur of the moment. Mr. Prager told me he would get in touch with me in a few days about my salary and other details, and we sealed the deal with a handshake. The first phone call I made with this exciting news was to Lucie.

A few days later, again during a busy time at the front desk, with countless guests vying for my attention, Mr. Prager called. He told me how much he was looking forward to working with me and offered me a salary. Preoccupied with my duties, I said yes.

A short time later I realized what absurd terms I had accepted: the salary he offered was very low. I also realized that he had probably expected me to negotiate a higher figure. But it was too late now. I had given my word.

My regrets vanished when I began the job a few weeks later. I was accepted with open arms by everyone at Mövenpick. I could see I was in for a real learning experience. The company was expanding rapidly and as a buyer I had access to all departments. This gave me insight into how decisions were made and how people on different levels of a business interacted. And I also had the opportunity to assist in opening new restaurants, including the one in Geneva.

I learned a lot from UP, as we called him. He was tough but kind-hearted. I was very fortunate to work with him on a daily basis for a couple of years.

There was one thing about UP that I considered unusual at the time but understood later when I was running my own business. UP had a policy that his company would pay its bills exactly on time. He gave our accounting department the necessary approval to pay the bills from accredited suppliers, but they were not allowed to file them until he had personally reviewed them.

I'll never forget those huge piles of bills stacked on the otherwise very tidy oak desk in his large, ornate office. UP would gaze at a pile as if he was in meditation. Then he would pull one bill out of the pile, look at it, then another one, and so on for maybe half an hour. He always found several mistakes: a late payment, a calculation error, a wrong price or quantity. Back the offending bills would go to the people who had authorized them for payment, accompanied by admonishing notes written in his shaky blue scrawl. This practice sent a message to everyone in the company: that the boss was watching and exercised personal control over the details of his business.

I was successful as a buyer and had a good personal relationship with UP and my colleagues, with one exception: Paul, the head of marketing. He seemed to have a problem with me, but I couldn't figure out what it was. I did nothing about it because I was extremely busy and he was never openly objectionable to me and never interfered with my work.

On the first day of my work at Mövenpick, I was put in charge of the new buying department. I had to report directly to UP. Mövenpick at the time was considered to be an interesting start-up company, and many suppliers wanted to have a business relationship with it at the very outset in order to beat their competition. This put me in a good position to find bargains for the company.

I thoroughly enjoyed the challenge of negotiating and the win-or-lose aspect of it. Of course, I didn't win all the time – that would have been boring – but I did attain a lot of experience in what was possible and what not, when to withdraw and when not. I realized that negotiating is above all a game of flexibility.

One trick helped me a lot. I have never told anybody about it until now. It was the easy-to-learn technique of reading upside down. I practiced for many hours by reading newspapers from a reverse position. I achieved such skill that I could easily read the notes of my negotiating partners, which often let me in on the limits they were working within.

At that time, smoked salmon and lobster were only available in exclusive restaurants at exorbitant prices. Ueli Prager had the idea of making these rarities, and other seafood, available to everybody at reasonable prices, and that is what garnered him a lot of publicity and made Mövenpick famous. I was in charge of buying the smoked salmon, and because we considered the quality from Denmark to be the best available, I made many enjoyable trips to that country to check quality and negotiate prices.

Another innovation made Mövenpick unique and contributed to its phenomenal success. At that time, restaurants served a warm meal only at lunch, between noon and two p.m., and then again for dinner. Mövenpick gave the public the opportunity to have a warm meal any time of the day.

What I learned
from this experience

1 Decisions need time.

I made some of my worst mistakes when I didn't take time to consider my options, as, for instance, when I said yes too quickly to the salary offer from my future boss. It took me a full year to make up for that one. Now I have a personal policy. Whenever I am too busy or preoccupied to give full attention to a matter, I automatically reply non-committally, saying something like, "May I call you back about this?" or "When would a good time be during the next few days to call you?"

2 A mentor is an entrepreneur's biggest asset.

Having a mentor, a coach, someone to look up to, is the best way for future entrepreneurs to learn. I learned a lot from such people at Mövenpick and elsewhere. But the time spent at Mövenpick was especially beneficial. I have always been grateful for how UP patiently answered my many questions. I don't think I would have become as successful as I did without his wisdom. Of course, I didn't realize this then – I was too young. But later in life it became clear to me that he had set an example for decision making that had helped me again and again.

3 Good bosses neither slumber nor sleep.

Of course you have to delegate when you're running a company. If you take responsibility for every task yourself, you'll fail spectacularly. However, it's a good idea to follow UP's example and retain control of the significant tasks. The way you handle such responsibilities tells your employees non-verbally who is boss. It teaches them some very important lessons, including professionalism, responsibility, care, concern for accuracy, and concern for customers and suppliers. These lessons will help them develop as workers and always think in terms of the interest of the company. When your employees know that you care about what's going on at the detail level, they will show loyalty to you by caring about details of their own work. That is a recipe for success.

A blessing
in disguise

MÖVENPICK was growing rapidly and UP decided to hire a management company to streamline our organization. This was just when Lucie and I had decided to get married. I informed UP of our plans, inviting him and his wife to the wedding. I also asked for a raise. I considered myself underpaid in relation to the huge transactions I was handling for the company. He promised that he would think about it and let me know.

UP and his wife attended our wedding and then Lucie and I were off on a three-week honeymoon in the French Riviera. During this wonderful time, I became very impressed with Lucie's business sense as we walked on the beach talking about my future with Mövenpick and what I could do to improve the buying department.

We arrived back late in Zürich on a rainy night that cruelly underscored the difference between Switzerland and the paradise we had just exited. I looked through the mail that had accumulated during our time away. There in the midst of the bills and best wishes from family and friends was a private letter from UP. I have to admit that I opened this letter first. I was sure I would find within it an announcement of a new salary or promotion.

The envelope contained a surprise all right: a pink slip, signed by Ueli Prager, my mentor and champion, the very person who had told me so many times how much he enjoyed working with me, who had complimented me on my job, and who had attended my wedding just three weeks earlier.

I was fired!

A wave of fear rolled right over me. How was I going to support Lucie without a job? I certainly didn't have much of a reserve in the bank. I was shaken that my idol had not even had the decency and courage to wait a few days and tell me the news personally. More than that, my lack of self-esteem and fear of authority, which I thought I had under control while I was working at Mövenpick, came back to haunt me. I knew I had to do something about it. It was at that time that I heard of psychoanalysis for the first time, though I did nothing about it.

The rumor mill told me that Paul in marketing had devised a plot against me during my absence. It must have been a good one for UP to fall for it.

All was not lost, as I was able to use my down time after being fired to propose a new and interesting job to a major company, and that job would lead directly to my becoming an entrepreneur.

Lucie was of invaluable help in such situations. She came from a similar background as mine and understood perfectly that an entrepreneur had to be totally committed to his company. He had to eat, drink, sleep, and breathe his business. It goes without saying that such a commitment required sacrifices. We were both ready to accept them.

Many years later, by this time a successful retailer myself, I accepted an offer from Mövenpick to sell their coffee and ice cream. We became a significant client of theirs and one day UP called me and invited me to lunch. The two of us dined on tenderloin at his restaurant in Zürich, on the first floor of the Mövenpick Dreikönig, passing the time pleasantly by talking shop. Finally, while we were waiting for our dessert and coffee,

I asked him the question that had been on my mind for many years.

"Mr. Prager, why . . . ?" was all I had to say. UP knew immediately what I was talking about. He hesitated, then told me that he had made a mistake by believing the wrong people. He said that when he found out he was wrong, he wanted me back. But by then it was too late.

"Letting go of you was one of my biggest mistakes," he said, looking me straight in the eye.

This made me feel very good. I returned his gaze and replied, "Although it was a difficult time then, I want to thank you for firing me. It turned out to be a blessing in disguise."

We parted as friends.

What I learned
from this experience

I Knowing how to let go is essential to business and life.

There is a time to be angry and a time to let go. I am thankful that even at my young age I was able to handle this experience by letting go and focusing on my future. I have to give tribute to my wife for this. She taught me to accept the past as a reality and focus on the really important thing: our future.

We have all had bad experiences. The trick is to recognize that these experiences will soon be part of history and that we cannot change them. The angrier we become, the more urgent it is for us to let go. Letting go of our bad experiences, our anger, our frustration, our lust for revenge is nothing other than an act of self-preservation and self-defence. I know from long experience that when we don't let go, we only hurt ourselves.

2 Don't give up.

That's easy to say, looking back today, but at the time being fired was devastating. My self-confidence was subterranean and the unanswered why question weighed heavily on my mind. Support from friends and family was vitally important. But eventually it was time to stop looking back, assess the situation bravely, and accept the fact that the situation was irreversible. Some people think that everything happens for a reason. In my case it was more than that: the situation was truly a blessing in disguise, as I will describe in the next story.

The first
Cash and Carry

WHILE I was a buyer at Mövenpick, I regularly went to trade shows, business association lunches, and other business events in order to meet people. Networking not only brought value to the company, it also helped me personally to know the main players in the business world.

Not long before being shown the door at Mövenpick, I was attending a boring marketing conference in Lugano in the Italian-speaking part of Switzerland. There were several guest speakers who couldn't seem to find the end of their speeches. Finally, under the influence of a particularly droning speaker, I could take it no longer and fell asleep. Just then I was saved from disgracing myself by the chairperson's forceful adjournment of the session. I was not only tired but also was hungry. I was pleased to see that the next item on the agenda was the banquet.

At the banquet I happened to sit down next to a very nice elderly gentleman who looked to be in his sixties. We exchanged introductions and I learned that he was Alois Job, the general manager of USEGO, Switzerland's largest food wholesale distribution company. In spite of his powerful position, he was an unassuming and pleasant man who seemed to be genuinely interested in his young lunchmate.

I met some very interesting people at these meetings and was always accepted in spite of my tender years, though it didn't hurt that I was a buyer for a fast-growing restaurant chain. The unspoken question in the minds of each of us at these meet-and-greet occasions was, "What can he do for me?" Eventually I became accustomed to this unspoken but realistic way that each of us evaluated the other.

But Mr. Job was different. He didn't talk about himself and his business. He was an excellent listener, asking my opinion on this and that.

To me it was just a pleasant lunch after a boring morning. I had no way of knowing how much that meeting would change my life.

Not long after this, while I was still working at Mövenpick, I came across an interesting article in a business magazine. It described a new type of store that had been opened exclusively in Scandinavia: a self-service wholesale store for retailers and restaurants, something not too different, in size, anyway, from today's Costco or Sam's Club but with only retail stores or restaurants as customers. Before this northern innovation, merchandise for food retailers or restaurants was delivered to the individual stores. In the new approach, the retailer himself could go and get his merchandise and therefore could get it cheaper because there were no transportation costs involved. What a fascinating concept!

A few days after my departure from Mövenpick, I remembered the article and I remembered Alois Job. I wrote a business plan for a chain of stores to which I gave the working title Cash and Carry. I telephoned Mr. Job, explained the idea to him, and suggested a meeting. At that meeting, I told him of my conviction that this new approach would spread over Europe. I very decently suggested that I would organize and open the first such store in Switzerland for his company. At this point I handed him my business plan. We would have to act fast, I told him. Time was of the essence. The competition would not wait. He told me that he would get back to me in a few days.

I was all keyed up and pretty sure that he would say yes. Although he hadn't made a commitment yet, I kept on planning. I thought about a location and made a rough design of the interior of the store. I also researched a new invention in which a computer punch-card system was used to streamline checkout and automatically keep track of inventory. And I indulged myself in a favorite hobby, designing a marketing plan.

Alois Job's call came the same week. He gave me his unconditional okay and a substantial budget. He had only one condition and on this he was adamant. It would be my responsibility to inform him weekly and in detail about the development of the project. Other than that, I was on my own. The trust he showed made me feel wonderful. I was happy to have the opportunity to build something new and significant for him and his company.

What a day that was! Less than a month after I was fired, I had a new and much more exciting job and a much better salary.

I immediately left for Sweden to research the first such store in full operation. I had been in Stockholm many times on buying trips for Mövenpick and had friends there, so it was easy for me to locate the new store and get the information I needed. Seeing the new idea in the flesh only made me even more aware of what a great idea it was. I was spellbound. I just couldn't understand why no one had ever thought of doing this before.

Back in Switzerland, I gave my findings in my next weekly report to my boss, emphasizing again that we had to act immediately. I received his final okay to proceed.

Work began immediately, in deep secrecy. It was a huge undertaking, considering that this kind of store didn't exist outside Scandinavia. Mr. Job helped me get over many internal blocks in his company. He never wavered in his support, and seeing how much he believed in me made me work all the harder. I also received strategic support from my wife, Lucie, who took care of all the paperwork at no charge.

One of our major innovations was above-mentioned system of keypunch cards, the forerunner of today's bar-coding systems. The idea was brand new at that time and generated a lot of interest. Every card had a code, made of holes in different places on the card, indicating the quantity per case, the price, the product number, the quantity in stock, and other information. We leased a first-generation computer that read such coding and automatically wrote the bill and subtracted the products from our inventory after they were sold.

The punch cards were located in a little box just below each product. The customer, when loading his shopping chart, took a corresponding number of punch cards with him. As we sold only original cases, it would be one per case. For instance, if the customer wanted to buy three cases of beer, he took three cards. When he had finished his shopping, we checked his cart and cards and the computer wrote the bill. This minimized our costs, helped us control our stock, and made us very competitive. The beauty of it was that we didn't need a separate warehouse – the store itself was the warehouse.

I found a location with ample parking on the outskirts of Zürich. After a very short time and supported by a media and advertising blitz, we opened the first Cash and Carry. It was a huge success from the very first day and it changed the way wholesalers and restaurants bought their merchandise. What added to the shopping experience was the fact that the Cash and Carry also became a social gathering place for all kinds of tradespeople in the food business.

A few months later, we opened our second store, this one in Egerkingen, close to the head office of the company. I was preparing to expand our formula for success accross the country, aware as I was that the competition was breathing down my neck.

And then something unexpected happened: Alois Job died,

after a short illness. This changed the whole picture. And not just because of my grief over losing a friend and a role model but also because the dynamic of his company changed radically. Thomas Carlyle, the famous historian, said that an organization is but the lengthened shadow of one man. I was seeing the truth of this for the first time.

The new manager was totally different from Mr. Job. It wasn't long before the freedom and support I enjoyed was taken away and a bureaucratic way of doing business imposed on me instead. Let's call this little Napoleon Mr. Blockman. Everything had to be submitted to him and approved by him and the process usually took a long time. We were not even allowed to buy office supplies without his consent. I often heard him proclaim his favorite expression, "It's my way or the highway."

People began leaving the company to find other jobs, and morale within the company sank like like a stone. I was very frustrated, too, but my fear of authority and lack of self-confidence made it very difficult for me to pursue my plan. But in spite of my insecurity, I thought I could go ahead with our plans, even under the new management, to expand to other cities. But Mr. Blockman blocked every attempt. Many times I heard him say, "I carry the responsibility and I decide and no one else – and my answer is no!" I needed all my courage to point out to him the phenomenal success of our first two stores. I emphasized that the competition was forming up to open the same kind of stores. But his no was insurmountable. Going from the support of Alois Job to the outright hostility of Blockman felt like falling off a high cliff from enthusiasm to despair.

Blockman was certainly not a skilful businessman. His response to my campaign with him was to create an administrative monster, a committee of eight people who were charged with the task of analyzing and brainstorming the Cash and Carry idea: its past, present, and future performance. They had no incentive to work quickly because he did not give them a deadline for their final report. That move stymied the project. I tried everything to make the Group of Eight work faster. I even became obnoxious, risking the loss of my job, but there was no way to speed up the monster.

Sure enough, I was forced to watch with frustration and disillusionment as one of our competitors, a small but very active company by the name of Angehrn, opened a similar discount store, then another. Another of our competitors opened one, too. We had given away our chance.

After six months of storming the barricades of the Group of Eight, I realized there was no way to win and left the company.

And what happened to USEGO, the once dominant player in the food wholesale business? USEGO never opened another Cash and Carry even though the two stores that I had opened continued to operate successfully. Blockman was replaced after a few years, but by then it was too late for USEGO to play a major role. The company was later sold and incorporated into another group of companies.

What I learned
from this experience

1 The power of networking.

A very important component of an entrepreneur's success, especially one who is just starting out, is networking. You have to know most of the players personally, especially your suppliers and your competitors. The best way to do so is to socialize through business associations, trade shows, and any kind of social gathering, be it in clubs, special-purpose groups, or other similar get-togethers.

Knowing the people and getting them to know you will help you solve many of the problems that will definitely come into your life as an entrepreneur. Agreed, these meetings are often boring and time-consuming and you don't always meet interesting people, but it is the only way to have access to the right people for the right time. It allows you to pick up the phone and talk directly to the person you need, instead of going through intermediaries.

2 The importance of being open to new ideas and keeping track of them.

When I read that article in a newspaper about the new concept of store in Sweden, I was immediately fascinated by the idea and stored it away in my brain for future reference if I needed it. And I did need it. The majority of my ideas I ended up not being able to use. But the few really good ideas that I had were extremely important. Opening your mind to new ideas – for marketing, for example, or for new developments – will help you keep a step ahead of the competition and defend your share of the market.

I learned to keep a folder that I named "New Ideas." Whenever I read something that sounded interesting, it went into the folder.

So many times when I reviewed the contents of that folder I came across an old idea that I had forgotten but that proved to be exactly what I needed.

3 How to pick the right people and double-check your picks.

The way Blockman treated me left a deep impression on me, not only because he frustrated my plans but also because I saw how much damage a Napoleon-type personality, supported by an inflated bureaucracy, can do to a firm. I don't know who hired Blockman, or how he sold himself to that person, but that one decision contributed directly to the company's demise. This did not have to happen. Active supervision of his performance by the board could have nipped it in the bud.

The Adventures of an Entrepreneur

Part Three

Introduction

WHEN I look back on my life to the point covered so far in this book, it feels to me like a series of stops and starts. I knew I wanted to be my own boss and I knew what I liked doing, but for the most part I just took whatever path presented itself to me, to see where it might lead.

During these years and on into the early years of the next stage of my life, becoming my own boss, I could not free myself of the problems I had to endure in my growing-up phase. In spite of my ongoing education, which enabled me to earn a diploma at the Hotel School and learn to speak four languages, in spite of the financial success of Cash and Carry, and in spite of invaluable help from my little rebel, I still had feelings of insecurity. I thought starting my own business would help me compensate for these feelings. But it wasn't as easy as that, as I will show later in this book in the story "Life on the Couch."

The years of actually being an entrepreneur, described in this part, had a very different feel to them – the feeling of getting on a circus ride and knowing that the only way to survive was to hold on for dear life until the damn thing finally stopped. The years spent starting and growing my food discount chain, PickPay, and the first computer store in Switzerland, Microspot, were far more exciting and fulfilling than I could have ever hoped. I was finally the master of my own fate – that is, if you don't count the vagaries of the market, the scheming of my competitors, the challenges of hiring the right people . . .

What's in
a name?

IN spite of the competition forming up as Blockman fiddled while USEGO burned, I decided I would start my own food discount store. The only silver lining in the cloud of my time at USEGO was that I had formed a business plan and put it into effect on someone else's tab. I had been allowed a series of rehearsals for what I was confident I could now perform on my own.

My wife and I were having difficulty coming up with a catchy name for our new venture. Everything else was falling into place. We had the concept, were zeroing in on where our first location would be, and were ready to unleash our marketing plan upon an unsuspecting public. But still, no name.

In spite of brainstorming with our friends, studying books that listed ideas for company names, asking for ideas from just about anyone who crossed our path, the right name just wouldn't present itself to us. I knew how important a name was. It had to stick in people's minds from the very first time they saw or heard it. But it also had to feel right to me personally for me to be absolutely committed to the enterprise it represented.

While waiting for divine inspiration, I took care of more terrestrial matters. I opened a numbered company, found a location, signed a lease, talked to banks and to private investors in search of capital – all without a final name for my new baby. I was stubborn and uncompromising on this matter.

One evening, some friends invited us over for dinner to meet guests of theirs from South Africa. In the midst of the usual dinnertime patter, one of the guests asked me what business I was in. When I said food retail, he mentioned that South Africa had a new and very successful discount chain by the name of Pick and Pay. I was electrified. My wife must have been, too, because she was playing footsie with me under the table. I was so excited that I choked and spilled wine all over the table. Lucie looked at me, I looked at her, and without a word we both knew that our company had just been named.

The next day we made sure that the name was not already registered. Seeing the way was clear, we changed the numbered company to Pick and Pay Inc. Now our baby could be introduced to the public.

But things are never finished until they're finished and even then they're not finished. A few months later, after we had already opened two Pick and Pay stores and were in the midst of an intense advertising campaign, I received a letter from a lawyer. He informed me that he represented a client by the name of Mr. Pick and that this Mr. Pick wanted us to stop using his name. We later found out that this man worked for one of our competitors – go figure! Our lawyer told us that Swiss law gave his suit a likelihood of success. Did I want to form up a countersuit in order to buy some time?

I had never met Mr. Pick and didn't want to be distracted by a lawsuit. I didn't even lose my temper. I just changed our name to PickPay, which was even catchier and passed the legal litmus test. We could have changed it back to Pick and Pay a few years later when Mr. Pick passed away, but by that time the name was branded – and the stores bear this name to this very day.

What I learned
from this experience

1 A lot's in a name.

One of the most important assets of any company is its name, because it gives immediate recognition. When I watch TV ads today I am often stunned by how little attention is given to products' and companies' names, by how much time is spent in stupid gags before the name is displayed. The all-important name often appears at the very end, when people are already tired of watching the commercial or have already clicked to another station.

Have you ever watched the TV commercial from Wal-Mart, one of the most successful companies in the world? They don't waste time with unrelated gags. They focus one hundred percent on two important messages: their brand name and the fact that they are always cheaper. All of the companies I founded had a catchy name and I believe that this was one of the major factors in their success. Try to imagine the phenomenal success of Apple's iPod without that fantastic name.

2 You make your own luck.

Agreed, we came across our name by a stroke of luck. But I believe that this stroke of luck occurred because we were confident we would eventually find the right name if we kept working on it and remained open to the right idea. We found this was also so in finding the right locations for our stores, the right marketing ideas, the right employees and management. Knowing the importance of a name, I refused to settle for a B-name while there was still the chance for an A-name.

3 Competitors should never be underestimated.

The more successful you are, the more of a target you will become for disruptive actions by competitors. In the story above, we were the target of a legal suit. Most of the time, however, this kind of thing happens behind the scenes. If your competitor is a powerful company, they may very quietly try to influence your suppliers or put other obstacles in your path. If this happens to you, don't be afraid, don't get angry, and don't seek revenge. Do take the attention as a compliment on your business skills. Ask yourself, could there be a better proof of my success?

Opening-day jitters

OPENING a store amid cutthroat competition was a risky undertaking. I was a virtual newcomer to this business of selling to the end-user. My experience was courtesy of the Cash and Carry stores, where we sold in bulk and exclusively to retailers and restaurants. But this time I didn't want to put any limits on who my customers could be. Everybody should be welcome. The problem was that I was widely unknown to the general public. And that I was living on borrowed money. I knew that the opening of the first PickPay discount store had to be memorable. This would be a make-or-break issue for our young company.

I spent a lot of time thinking about the right promotion. But nothing I thought of seemed interesting enough. With the opening date – appropriately enough, we had chosen December 6, which is St. Nicholas Day in Europe – coming up fast, I grew more and more tense.

Then I had *the* idea, an idea for something that had never been done before. I called it "When the Bell Rings Everything Is Free." Here is how I set it up. I installed a clock to be used just on opening day, setting it to ring three times every hour. Whoever was at checkout when it rang would get everything in his or her shopping cart for free. It goes without saying that I picked a clock with an ear-shattering alarm. I didn't want just the people in our store to hear it; I wanted everyone in the shopping mall where the store was located to hear it, too.

There was just one problem: there were strict laws in the country at the time against lotteries, and my little gambit could well be considered a lottery.

I went to see my lawyer for advice.

"As your lawyer I have to advise you not to go ahead with your idea," he said. "I understand that it is a great marketing pitch, but you risk getting into trouble with the police. They might even close your store."

Then he paused and a pensive look came over his face. He leaned back in his chair and said, "A discussion is going on right now about repealing this law, but at this time it is still in effect. Well, the decision is yours and of course we would help you if there were any problems . . ."

Did I really see him wink at me?

As far as I was concerned, the importance of grabbing the public's attention on opening day trumped whatever legal exposure we might have.

I had the clock set by a notary public so that no one, not even I, would know when it was going to ring. I knew this would help my case if I ran into legal difficulties.

Was I nervous? Of course I was. I had a severe case of opening-day jitters. After all, it was my very first store and it was important that we did things right. If this store didn't succeed, that would be it. I did not have the financial means to pursue my dream of being an entrepreneur beyond this. Risk taking – calculated risk taking – was the name of the game. So we placed full-page ads in the local papers, enticing people with the prospect of free goods.

The reaction was overwhelming.

An hour before the store opened, a line of people was forming at the door, and it kept growing until at opening time there were about 200 customers waiting to get in, accompanied by several reporters and cameramen.

I was very proud of our success and flaunted it a bit as I opened the door. I saw this as the first day of many, many happy days at our stores. But when I opened the door, my smile disappeared. The first customers to walk in were two police officers. After introducing themselves, they explained my offense and told me that they had no alternative but to close the store right then.

The people behind them were growing restless. I politely took the officers aside to argue my case with them – of course thereby allowing the customers to storm past them into the store. As I talked to the officers, people roamed freely all over the store, to the accompaniment of media flashlights and TV camera lighting.

"But you can't be serious," I said to the officers. "Look at all these people shopping here."

"Sorry, but we're just following orders," they said.

I suggested that they call their supervisor and tell him about the huge crowd and the media. They did so and apparently received new orders, because after hanging up they politely bade us farewell and left.

By the end of that first day, the store was empty of merchandise. I did not realize that this was just the beginning of what would become a very successful chain of PickPay stores. But I know now that such a thing would never have happened without my audacious promotion.

A few months later, I learned that no court case would be forthcoming. I had to pay a fine, and shortly after that the law was repealed.

I'll never forget one very special incident from that day. Before we decided to go into business for ourselves, my wife worked as a personal secretary to a wealthy businessman. This good man wanted to support us on our first day of business. He stood patiently in line and then went through the store filling three shopping carts with food. Of course, as often happens to good people, the bell rang exactly when he was checking out. He did not want to accept the freebies, but we persuaded him to do so and he reluctantly accepted. I learned later that he gave the amount he had saved to charity.

What I learned
from this experience

1 To follow my goal and not let anyone distract me.

At that time I was in my mid-thirties and the successful store opening jump-started my career as an entrepreneur. It was my persistence and determination to follow my goals and not let anyone distract me from achieving them that made the difference. That may have meant that some people found me opinionated and pushy, but my desire to succeed took priority for me. As a then-unknown businessperson with a new company name, working in a tough business environment, a successful store opening that would get people talking was of vital importance. Everything else paled in comparison.

2 To take risks – calculated ones.

There is no entrepreneurial success without taking risks. The solution is not to avoid risks but to minimize their potential for damage. I learned quickly not to take them just for the fun of it. They always had to be calculated risks. Of course, the risk that I took could have gone wrong. An unsuccessful opening would have been the end of my dream of becoming an entrepreneur. It was vitally important, therefore, for me to assess the risk accurately and include other people's opinions in my decision making. In hindsight, it turned out that my assessment was right and that I had interpreted my lawyer's wink correctly. However, that was not enough. I invested a lot of time in evaluating what could go wrong and how important that was in comparison with my goal.

David and
(a nice) Goliath

EARLY in our deliberations we had a brainwave. We decided to locate our first PickPay in Zürich – in Oerlikon, at the Bauhof, right above an outlet of one of Switzerland's largest and most successful companies, Migros.

Migros was founded in 1925 by the late consumer-rights advocate, Gottlieb Duttweiler, an exceptional personality. Since then it has evolved into a co-operative and is the number-one retailer and the largest employer in Switzerland. Its empire includes well over 500 stores, including supermarkets, convenience stores, and department stores. It also includes banking and insurance operations, health clubs, a printing and publishing company, and restaurants, along with other endeavors. Over the years since 1925, Migros has spread from its home country to many other places in Europe.

Besides size, there was one major difference between PickPay and Migros: the way we approached the marketplace. We both sold groceries and related products to the end-user, but PickPay sold nothing but national-brand products and Migros sold nothing but their own private labels. And there was one other difference.

Migros didn't sell alcohol or tobacco but we had a big department selling these products.

Vastly different though we were, I couldn't get it out of my head what a fantastic match PickPay and Migros could be. Locating our stores close to their high-traffic stores could bring us customers, and their customers, meanwhile, would benefit from being able to buy their private brands and our national brands at virtually one and the same time.

But like most dreams, this one didn't make sense, at least not on the face of it. I was warned by friends that my idea would not work. After all, PickPay and Migros were competitors, targeting the same customers. Competitors don't co-operate, they fight!

A few months later, I was invited by a representative from Migros to meet with their management. The meeting took place in Rüschlikon, right outside of Zürich, where Migros had donated to the general public a recreational park that was named after the founder of the company. There was a restaurant in this Gottlieb Duttweiler Institute, and that is where we had lunch.

What an interesting meeting it turned out to be. It was kind of like David and Goliath – only in this case the large and powerful Goliath turned out to be kind and friendly to the smaller David. This group had many questions about my business, my marketing philosophy, and my reasons for choosing my location just above their supermarket. I quickly realized that they were testing me. I decided to take full advantage of this opportunity to sell them on my concept of the benefits both parties could enjoy by marketing to the same customers.

Imagine my surprise to find out that I didn't really have to sell my idea to them. They had done their homework. They knew everything about Bruno Gideon and his PickPay stores. They, too, realized the benefits of our stores being in close proximity to theirs. They indicated that they would think about it but pointed out that any form of co-operation could never be made public.

Shortly afterward, I was contacted by Mr. Stiller from the

Migros real estate department. He offered me the opportunity to rent a store in a new shopping mall where Migros was opening a large supermarket. Our store would thus be located in a new shopping mall in the fast-growing suburb of Zürich-Altstetten that would certainly attract lot of new customers. I accepted enthusiastically. That would be store number three for us.

But then, ever the restless entrepreneur, I had another idea. In order to build upon our co-operation, I advertised PickPay on local buses and streetcars in and around Zürich using this catch phrase:

PickPay – the "migros" of National Brands

I put the name Migros between quotation marks and intentionally lowercased the first letter to make it clear that it was not their advertisement.

This campaign cost me an arm and a leg but seeing those advertisements on the sleek blue buses and streetcars plying the busy city streets brought a big smile to my face. That smile only grew bigger when I saw an immediate increase in business.

While I was pleased as punch with my marketing idea, Migros was anything but. A few days after the launch of my campaign, I was contacted again by Mr. Stiller. During a lunch meeting at a casual Italian restaurant in the heart of Zürich, this nice, jovial man in his mid-fifties delicately approached what turned out to be the real reason for our get-together: my advertisement. I can still remember our remarkable discussion and the way he handled it.

"I would like to personally compliment you on your latest marketing idea," he began. "It certainly draws the customer's attention to the fact that he can buy national brands and our products in one trip. Very good thinking."

Before I could thank him for the compliment, he continued, still with a pleasant smile, "There is only one problem. Our marketing department doesn't like how you are using both names together. They would like to see the campaign terminated immediately. They asked me to contact you and share their thoughts with you. Of course, the final decision is yours."

Mirroring his warm and friendly smile, I answered, "Thank you for your kind observations. But I am confident that your marketing department will change their minds as soon as they realize how much Migros benefits from the free publicity this advertising campaign will give them."

He responded, "Well, that may be. However, knowing them, I wouldn't count on it. I don't know this for a fact, but I have heard through the grapevine that they have contacted the company's lawyers regarding this matter."

We chatted some more and I relayed my excitement about the new stores I was being invited to open next to their supermarkets. We concluded our lunch on friendly terms.

Today, I am stunned by my reaction and my courage. What could have made me think I could insult a multi-billion-dollar company by not taking their wishes seriously? How could I have been so oblivious to Mr. Stiller's veiled threat about lawyers? At the time I was nothing but a tiny player with a young company, still wet behind the ears. They could have crushed me in a split second. However, I was in my thirties and felt empowered by the success of the first of my stores. I felt invincible.

But they didn't crush me and their reaction was a huge learning experience for me. A few days later, Mr. Stiller called and we had lunch again at the same restaurant. I have to admit that I was a bit nervous. He waited until the end of the lunch to touch on the subject.

"I reported to the marketing people about our last meeting," he said, again with a friendly smile. "They asked me to contact you again and present you with their point of view. They haven't changed their minds and would like you to take the advertisements down immediately. And they also asked me to tell you that our company will not put any pressure on you – that would be against our beliefs in a free market – and that the decision is entirely yours. But I personally would be happy if the relationship between our two companies could continue."

Despite his friendly manner, Mr. Stiller looked at me meaningfully. When I did not reply, he put back into his briefcase, in a this-matter-is-closed manner, a folder clearly marked as containing prospective sites for additional PickPay stores close to Migros neighborhoods.

At that moment the potential growth of further co-operation hit me with full force. I realized that I was being stubborn about a trivial matter. Message received. I told him that I would cancel the ads the next day. Mr. Stiller thanked me for my positive response and we parted.

A week later, I was invited to rent space next to another Migros outlet, and about a year later, I was selected to have the only discount store in Switzerland's largest shopping mall, the huge Glattzentrum outside Zürich, in which Migros was a major partner. Although it was never made definite who was helping me behind the scenes, I have no doubt that it was Migros.

I remember the opening day of this huge shopping mall. My promotion that day didn't make me many friends among my competitors. I had ordered T-shirts emblazoned with the words, "PickPay is cheaper – always!" I assembled many employees from our other stores and asked them just to walk around the mall, wherever they wanted, wearing the T-shirts. This action provoked some angry comments and complaints from the other stores. When the manager of the shopping center intervened, he did so with an impish smile on his face and only after the parade was over.

What I learned
from this experience

1 The importance of finding the right pitch.

One of the most important points to ensure the success of a new venture is the pitch. Ask yourself the question, "What makes my business different from all other competitors?" Then try to state this difference in as concise a sentence as possible. The pitch is not easy to come up with. It requires a lot of brainstorming and thinking. But once you have it, it will be your most important message for marketing your business.

I had two pitches. One was "PickPay is cheaper – always!" and the other one was "PickPay – the 'migros' of National Brands." After I gave in to Migros's "request," I focused entirely on the other slogan.

2 The importance of not taking no for an answer.

I was impressed by the high level of diplomacy that Migros exercised to get their way. Considering that they were a powerful company and I was just a small, insignificant start-up, this is very remarkable and shows their high level of ethics. They could have used force, an ultimatum, lawyers, and other such power moves to get their way but used diplomacy instead. They didn't even use their most powerful argument, namely that I had broken our agreement that our co-operation would not be made public.

What did I learn from their approach? Since then I have tried to avoid using force to get my way. I realized that "Migros diplomacy" is a much more powerful approach. In fact, my experience with the benevolent Goliath was what gave me the idea to write a book, *Don't Take No for an Answer!* (As an entrepreneur, I just can't avoid this good marketing opportunity: The book is available through major bookstores in Canada and the U.S. and Amazon.com and my website www.brunogideon.com.)

3 The importance of listening to my inner voice.

The first slogan – "PickPay is cheaper – always!" – was widely discussed internally and externally. Some of my employees and friends, along with some consultants, told me to change it. They felt that the word "cheap" would imply that the company was cheap. I didn't agree and used the slogan the entire time I advertised the stores. Gut instinct told me that I should continue using "cheap" because that is the word that people commonly use. Listen to your inner voice. If it is speaking to you strongly enough, you have no reason to change your opinion.

Breaking
the boycott

ONE of the most frustrating problems in the start-up phase of PickPay was the fact that distributors of well-known international brands, such as Juvena, L'Oreal, Fisher Price toys, and others, boycotted us. Although the system of controlled prices was officially over in Switzerland, they refused to sell to us unless we agreed to abide by their selling prices. Being discounters at heart, we could never agree to that. They tried everything to bring us to reason, from adulation to bribery, from compliments to lawyers' letters. Finally, when they saw we weren't going to budge, they refused to discuss the issue any longer and didn't even return our phone calls. The war was on.

I had a hunch that selling Fisher Price toys at half price for Christmas would be a great idea, not only for customers but also for PickPay's profile. But Fisher Price didn't think so. As soon as they heard, via the grapevine, about our intentions, they informed every seller of their products that selling to PickPay would get them expunged from their list of regular sellers.

Then it hit me that Fisher Price was a U.S. product. My brother, Walter, and his family lived there, so maybe he could get me around my problem. His business was distantly related to retail stores – he sold security devices to them.

"Get whatever you can," I urged him, "no limitation as to the quantity."

About three weeks later, he called me. "I have a surprise for you," he said with a laugh. "Guess what it is?"

I had no idea, but he was right: I was very surprised.

"I just received two truckloads full of Fisher Price toys. I am going to send them to Switzerland right away."

A few weeks later, and just in time for Christmas sales, I received the shipment, took out some full-page ads, and offered the toys at half price.

It was a big success for us, but a major annoyance to Fisher Price. They figured out from the serial numbers where the merchandise came from, but it was too late – there was nothing they could do.

I also decided to sell some of the best-known cosmetic products, such as Hairspray Elnett from L'Oreal, Sunscreen by Juvena, and a very prominent but overpriced hairspray by the name of Chandor. The only question was how we could get these products in sufficient quantities on the "black market." It proved to be less difficult than I thought, thanks to a human variable that came to my help: greed.

Mark Battaglia owned a hair salon near my office. He had cut my hair for many years and over time we had become good friends. One day, when we were alone in his barber shop, I asked if he could help me with a problem that was very confidential. I went on to tell him about the boycott.

"That is no problem at all," he said with a laugh. "I will be more than happy to help you." Then he continued, with a mischievous smile on his face, "As a matter of fact, I have some issues with these companies myself and would love to pay them back for what they did to me."

I never found out what he was talking about, but whatever it was, I had found an ally.

"I have many friends in the trade," he said. "I'll contact them and see what I can do."

I thanked him and repeated that the matter had to be treated with the utmost discretion because the distributors were as sharp as tacks.

A few days later, on a Friday afternoon, I received a phone call from Mark and we met that same evening at his shop, after it was closed. Mark told me he had found some "friends" who were willing to sell me these products at their cost price plus a small commission. He said that he would also like to be paid for the time he had invested in making the contacts and assembling the merchandise. He stressed that purchasing from his friends would have to be on a cash-on-delivery basis.

It turned out that the so-called small commission his friends required was a substantial one. But I agreed to pay it, without a second thought.

I agreed to meet Mark a week later, late at night, to get the hair-spray and whatever else he could provide, and pay the cash. The whole thing was risky, but I was young and high-spirited.

In order for Mark to call me at the office without raising suspicion, he used the name "Mr. Friday," the day of all his deliveries. I was stunned by the quantities he had been able to assemble and complimented him.

"No problem," he said. "There is much more where this comes from, but we'll have to wait. We don't want them to become too suspicious."

I took the whole lot to my apartment, which didn't thrill my wife, Lucie.

Interestingly, although everything was handled in total secrecy, word got around and more and more drugstores, spas, and hair salons wanted a piece of the action of getting supplies to us. There was the man we gave the name Forest Ranger, because the first time I met him was in a forest. Another we called Mr. Oliver, the name of his dog.

After a few weeks, when there was no longer any more room in our apartment, I decided to go ahead with our plan. All I had to do was place an ad in the major newspapers and offer the products at half their regular price. It was a huge success and the talk of the town for days.

An interesting incident happened when a spa, probably inspired by the distributor, tried to buy all the hairspray in the store. I happened to be on the floor when this attempt was made and shot a picture of the two men who were loading the wares in their shopping cart. Apparently they had not seen the sign that said, "Limit, two per person." I thought about how a picture of them would provide me with fantastic advertising. I could already see the photo caption, "Our prices are so low that even Spas buy at PickPay."

I suppose it was inevitable. Our competitor sued us for price-cutting, a ridiculous action that, in my opinion, had no other purpose but to block us. The suit, of course, didn't go anywhere and was withdrawn after one preliminary session in court.

I had forgotten one odd aspect of the case until it came back to me to me this very moment. I was at the courthouse with my wife, waiting to be called into court. The plaintiff walked into the hallway with his lawyer, a woman by the name of Helga. When she took off her coat, we saw that she was wearing exactly the same suit as my wife. When Lucie saw her double, she couldn't refrain from laughing. Helga turned her back to us. She was not amused.

Shortly after this, fixed prices were definitely abolished in Switzerland. Over time, our relationship with the distributors got back to normal, influenced in part by the growing volume of their products being sold in our stores.

I'm pleased to close this story with a memory that shows how broken bridges can be repaired. Eventually we had an excellent relationship with all of these companies, except for Fisher Price. In fact, year after year, the rep from L'Oreal gave a Christmas gift to my wife, a prestigious Hermès shawl. She treasures them to this very day.

What I learned
from this experience

1 Losing money can be beneficial.

I was determined to break the boycott and sell the national brands at a discount, even though, considering what I had to pay to Mr. Friday, the Forest Ranger, and Mr. Oliver, this would end up being below my cost. Was losing this money a wise thing to do? Yes. The publicity was well worth the price. There is no better publicity for a discounter than having the absolutely cheapest price in town.

2 Never to assume a relationship is over.

There is a time for war and a time for peace. After the action was over I waited a few months and then sent messages to the distributors that our doors were open and that we were interested in talking. I purposely never used that picture I shot in order not to insult individuals and make enemies unnecessarily. My calls for peace were heard by most of the companies concerned, and we ended up becoming good business partners and in some cases even friends.

The
search warrant

I was a quiet afternoon in our offices. We were all quietly performing our tasks when suddenly and without any warning, four local police officers entered and headed straight for my desk without greeting anyone. I stood up and asked if I could help them, but apparently they had not come in to chat. Instead, they presented me with a search warrant.

You can imagine my shock at having the police come to search our offices. I was even more shocked when it dawned on me that they planned to stay for hours or maybe even days. I had no idea what they were looking for. Was one of my employees in trouble? Had I done something wrong without realizing it?

At that time there were strict laws regulating retail in Switzerland. I had often pushed the envelope to assure the success of my company. However, I had never done anything illegal and had very little experience with the police. But the reality was that they were here and were not going anywhere.

They went through our file cabinets, inspecting and confiscating files and asking many questions. Although I always was a bit afraid of authorities – a relic of my experiences growing up – I gathered the courage to ask them why they were here, what they were looking for, and who had initiated the search. They refused to answer my questions and quietly went on with their work, which made me even more nervous.

At this point, our PickPay food discount stores had developed into a chain of six stores. We were doing very well. Our main competitor was a large and powerful company by the name of Denner. We had focused on quietly building our company (with the exception of my sporadic marketing splashes) because we didn't want them to know how well we were doing. However, I knew that they would eventually notice our growing market share and put some obstacles in our way.

I suspected that this moment had just come. I knew that if I didn't react immediately, Denner might gain access to our highly confidential buying information.

I called my lawyer, Eric Teitler, who immediately came to the store, but there was nothing he could do once a judge had issued a warrant. The next day, however, he protested the search warrant and the actions of the police. He asked the court to order all of the documents to be sealed until we had an opportunity to react. The motion was granted.

My suspicion proved to be correct. Denner was behind this action and for a ridiculous reason. Denner was a powerful company that ran full-page newspaper ads every week. In order to be competitive, I had made a decision to undercut the company in sales of some important brands, such as Coca-Cola. Karl Schweri, the owner of the company, made it so easy for me because he always advertised the same products at the same discount prices in the same paper on the same day every week. So naturally we always advertised the same product the same day in the same newspaper – at a lower discount. Apparently that did not sit well with him. It is still not clear to me how he had been able to get the wheels of justice moving with not even a scintilla of evidence.

The matter petered out over the next few weeks when the

police found nothing related to espionage. The investigation was closed. People urged me to throw a countersuit at him, but for some reason or other I never did. Maybe the reason was that I didn't want my secret to get out.

And what was my secret? No espionage, no tricks of any sort, just plain information gathering. A friend of ours lived in the neighborhood where my competitor had its warehouse. She would call us whenever big trucks drove up with basic goods such as Coca-Cola, washing detergent, toilet paper, or other bulk merchandise. Thus we always knew that a campaign for these products was in the offing. In the food discount game, nobody fills up a warehouse with such large quantities for no good reason. It was logical for us to conclude that they were meant to be sent to stores immediately. As his ads were always on a Tuesday, I knew what product to stack up in my store and what prices to put on it. The system worked for many more years. He never found out.

What I learned from this experience

1 To never underestimate my competitor.

In my naiveté and inexperience, I never imagined that a competitor would try to push me out of the market. Of course, not every competitor would do that, but I was lucky that nothing ever happened before the incident described above. From then on, however, I was very careful, discussing with my lawyer every out-of-the-box advertising campaign that I organized. Better safe than sorry.

2 To always show my strength.

Looking back from today's optics, I think that it might have been a mistake not to sue my competitor for damage. It would have given him the message, "So far and no further." He considered my not doing so to be a sign of weakness and continued his attacks against me, only on another level. Using his huge volume, he put pressure on our suppliers to prevent them from giving me good buying opportunities. He was successful only in a few cases – which of course I used as fodder for further publicity.

My Board
of Critics

THERE is a danger that sooner or later catches up with every entrepreneur: thinking inside the box. When you are consumed with numerous daily problems and working 24/7, you don't have much time and energy to step back and ask yourself, "Where are we now? Where will we be in five years? What are our weaknesses and strengths?" Thinking inside the box is the main reason that so many companies fail.

I was determined to avoid this risk. From the very first day of PickPay, I applied an open-door policy. Employees could drop by my office any time to let me know their thoughts on how the business was going. We invited feedback from all quarters: our workers, our customers, other people in the industry. We were especially open to new marketing ideas, which we knew were the lifeblood of any business.

Our employee suggestion system was almost a whole organization of its own, with promotions run and money paid for the best new ideas. This system had an important effect on our growth by helping our employees feel part of the PickPay family.

However, I clearly felt the need for advice from people from outside the box – from professionals and other analytical people.

I owned the company myself, so I didn't have a board of directors. There was an advantage to this. I had great freedom to follow my ideas. I could respond to marketing trends very quickly because there were no layers of authority to go through for approvals. But there was a disadvantage to this, too. I didn't have the benefit of supervision that such a board could provide. I needed what I called a "correction factor." But I thought of a way to redress that imbalance by forming a Board of Critics made up of some customers, some manufacturers, and some friends, all of them thoughtful and analytical in nature.

The purpose of this board was to scrutinize our performance from every angle and make observations of our policies and practices. A lot of good ideas came from that board.

But over time even that reservoir of ideas ran dry. We were growing extremely fast, so I began looking for professional advice. The main problem we faced was the $64,000 question, "Is it time for us to get a warehouse and have our own shipping force?" The reason the question came up was that our manufacturers were putting pressure on us. Understandably, they wanted to deliver the goods to one place instead of individual stores – and we were up to more than ten stores by this point. Still, had we really reached the point where we needed to invest heavily in such infrastructure?

One of the best consulting agencies, if not the top one in the world, is McKinsey. I had met one of their managers, Walter Abegglen, a friendly and communicative person, at a corporate luncheon. It was a pleasure to exchange ideas with him. I was impressed by his personality and was convinced that he was a highly qualified consultant. So I called him and invited him for lunch, at which I asked straight off whether McKinsey would do some research for us and advise us on the warehouse question.

Walter listened to me and his answer was remarkable. He probably should have turned my request down immediately, because we were a tiny company compared with his usual customers. But the way he concealed his "no" was remarkable and is worth repeating here. (What I was thinking as he spoke is in brackets.)

He looked at me with a smile and said, "Great idea and that would be an interesting job (*first say some nice words*), but McKinsey is a worldwide company and deals only with large corporations, most of them international (*give a reason to prepare the listener for the no*). You have done a remarkable job creating PickPay and I compliment you on this (*throw in some flattery*). However, at this time you are still a small company and our fee is at a level that you are not used to paying (*give the hearer a reason to accept the no*). I believe that you could use that money more beneficially for some interesting marketing activities. I would be glad to help you there. And I would do it privately and would charge only a small fee (*make it impossible not to accept the no*)."

It so happened that I have always been fascinated by the word "no" and later even wrote a book about it.* I am sure that you will not be surprised that I did not accept his no. Here is how I turned it around. I suggested that he could do basic research on a new and interesting topic, "the threshold problem in growing companies." I implied that this might open a new market for his company. He could use our company as an example. We would open our books to him, give him all the numbers, and help him with our knowledge of the market. Furthermore, he could publish the report, thereby showing that his company wasn't dealing exclusively with big names but also supported growing companies.

That did it. He wanted a few days to discuss the idea with his colleagues. I felt sure he would accept my suggestion and I was right. We talked later in the week and agreed on a fee that I considered very fair. He passed the job on to Klaus, one of his interns.

Working with McKinsey was an exceptional and very interesting experience. It was an object lesson in how real professionals work. Klaus listened patiently to the information we gave him.

---

* The title of the book is *Don't Take No for an Answer!* As a card-carrying entrepreneur, I had to mention it again.

"I have to double-check everything," he said. "No offense meant. These are my rules that I have to abide by."

The four of us – Lucie and I and Walter and Klaus – had regular meetings to discuss an agenda that Klaus had prepared. And Klaus really did find some mistakes in the way we were doing things, which justified his professional doubts.

The final report stated that we should not invest in a warehouse and should not have our own delivery trucks. I followed Klaus's suggestions right to the day I eventually sold PickPay, years later. The money I paid to McKinsey, though substantial, saved me much, much more.

Around the same time, I heard through the grapevine that Daniel Collins, founder and owner of the prestigious advertising agency Collins Partners Ltd. in Basel, had sold his company and was offering his experience and know-how as a marketing consultant. How could I resist such an opportunity? I called him and told him that we were interested in hiring him for a consulting job. We agreed to meet in one of our stores.

I will never forget that first (and last) meeting with Mr. Collins. He arrived in a Rolls Royce, complete with chauffeur. He greeted me brusquely and asked me to walk him through the store. It was customary in all our stores to keep the supplies above the shelves. This was very practical for replenishing empty shelves and gave our stores a warehouse-like appearance. Mr. Collins, without losing any time asking questions, pointed to the top of the shelves and said harshly, "This has to go. Find another place to store your boxes."

Then he went on to other issues, criticizing the displays, the layout, and practically everything else. At first I was annoyed, but then I thought how odd this was, a consultant who passed judgment on things he obviously didn't understand. I became intrigued with how he could have become such a prominent marketing guru. So I began asking him some questions.

As I learned more about him, my anger subsided and I felt

sorry for him. It turned out that Collins was used to working exclusively in teams. In his company, all the research, the marketing, and the initial contacts had been implemented by his directors and their assistants. Evidently he had not realized how dependent he had become on others. I could see that there was no way he was going to succeed in his new business if he didn't adjust, and fast. He was used to thinking inside the box and knew no other way.

I later learned that Collins had become seriously ill and had stopped acting as a consultant. There is no doubt in my mind that the frustrations he had to endure had become unbearable to him.

What I learned
from this experience

1 The necessity of thinking outside the box.

I am convinced that many excellent ideas are buried below the surface of the workforce. It is very important and fulfilling to dig them out. However, it is difficult to get above the daily routine of business life. Some try to do so by going on work-vacations, but that is rarely enough. I chose another way: my Board of Critics and a well-developed employee suggestion system that forced me to deal with the problems at hand.

2 How to turn a no into a yes.

Entrepreneurs do not have the vast research and development and consulting budgets of the big corporations. But they have the same, or even greater, need for outside viewpoints. The opportunities for professional advice are there, but you have to work at making good on them. Learning how to turn a no into a yes is therefore of vital importance.

3 Listen first, act later.

It didn't matter that Daniel Collins had an attitude or lost a consulting job. He probably didn't have to work anyway. But his example showed me how important it is to listen first and act later. That is the only way to be successful in a new challenge and to accept the change that comes with it. Doing so helps you avoid the ever-present danger of losing touch with reality.

Life on
the couch

MY Board of Critics helped me with external matters: store policies, marketing processes, expansion, and so on. But before even going into business on my own – when I was in my thirties and working at USEGO putting the Cash and Carry concept together – I realized that I needed someone to help me with internal matters. I'm talking about the state of my mind and soul. I was to learn that this process would become even more important to me both personally and entrepreneurially.

By the time I left Kefikon Boys' School, at age seventeen, I had become hardened, yet at the same time I was intimidated by and fearful of others, especially those in authority. Having been a victim for so long, I was in danger of becoming a victimizer. I had developed strong feelings of aggression but could not allow myself to act on them for fear of punishment. Somehow I was able to maintain my sense of vitality, but the fear of punishment hung like a cloud over my head. It is miraculous that in spite of this I was able to "catch up," learning many of the things about people and life and myself that I had missed while I was an adolescent. What saved me was my determination to invest time and money in my continuing education – both intellectual and emotional. All the time that I was working as an apprentice at Coop, studying and working in the hospitality business, and in the employ of Movenpick and USEGO, I was devouring books, attending countless seminars, and learning other languages, in the process earning several diplomas.

But education was not enough. The tension, the fear of authority, the uncertainty, and the lack of self-confidence, although hidden from other people, were still there. I was aware that my internal turmoil would make it difficult for me to be successful in my own business.

At that point a friend of mine suggested that I could get rid of these shortcomings by undergoing psychoanalysis. I turned to several books to study the subject, learning that it was a process I would have to commit to for many years. Did I really want that?

My friend recommended that I talk to several psychoanalysts and gave me some names. The first person I interviewed was Dr. Fritz Morgenthaler, a very prominent psychoanalyst of the Freudian school as well as a successful author and a professor at the University of Zürich. He was a gentleman in his late forties. He asked a lot of questions and I asked a lot of questions but my questions were not answered immediately. The good doctor used the old trick of answering a question with another question. I didn't like him at all, but what he said made sense. He explained that our emotions and behavior are often determined by subconscious factors over which we have no control, and that these factors create unhappiness, stress, difficulties in work or in relationships, or disturbances in mood and self-esteem.

"These forces are very strong," he said calmly, "but because they are subconscious, the advice of friends and family, the reading of self-help books, or even the most determined efforts often fail to bring relief. But in psychoanalysis we can bring these problems to the conscious level, which will allow you to deal with them."

This all sounded good, but I still did not like him, and after an hour I said goodbye, telling him that I might call. Looking back, I wonder whether it was my little rebel who didn't like him because he sensed he might lose his playground.

So I went to see another psychoanalyst, Dr. Sam Brown, a very nice and friendly man whom I liked from the very beginning. He also asked a lot of questions and explained that the process could take up to three years. I would have to come in for sessions three to four times a week, he said.

"You would have to vocalize everything that comes to your mind, unfiltered and without withholding anything, and we would together clear the backlog. This would allow you to access your deeper problems in a way that is not possible through any other method."

I asked Dr. Brown when we could start. His answer was disappointing.

"I would like to work with you, but at the moment I have no openings," he said. "If you could wait for a year, I believe I could accommodate you, but unfortunately not before." Then he added, "You'll find this problem with any good analyst. We are very busy."

I went to see two more practitioners, but guess where I eventually landed? Back with Dr. Morgenthaler. He happened to have an opening and this time I told my little rebel what to do, not the other way around.

I went to see Dr. Morgenthaler three times every week, for an hour each time. I had to lie on a couch while he sat at his desk behind me, out of my vision. My sole task was to talk. Talk about whatever came into my head: my experiences at Kefikon, my anger toward my parents, and all the other clouds that loomed over me. No dialogue this, not by any stretch of the imagination. I talked about myself to myself and Dr. Morgenthaler listened, hardly saying a thing. I often became angry with him, shouting at him and then apologizing and shouting again. In the sessions I was in a permanent conflict with my past, which I transferred to the doctor.

My little rebel didn't make life easy for us. I remember one time I was so angry that the analyst wouldn't answer my questions that I jumped up and stormed out of the room – only to return for the next session. Another time I asked him a question and when he didn't answer, I said, "I am not going to say one more word until you answer my question" and I was silent right to the end of the session.

Dr. Morgenthaler worked intensively with dreams. I had to write mine down, which became an interesting way to analyze my subconscious. I learned a lot about dream analysis and use it even today. Another important thing was free association. By voicing whatever came to my mind, I gave him fodder for determining the origin of my problems. He was then able to refine, correct, and add additional thoughts and feelings.

All the while, I wrestled with these insights, going over them again and again and experiencing them in my daily life, in fantasies, and in dreams. Slowly, once I had acted out my initial anger and frustration, Dr. M and I worked to clear away the bad experiences that were the base of my problems.

Dr. M *finally* began to give me his opinion. His voice was always maddeningly calm and I didn't always agree – or shall I say that my little rebel didn't always agree – with his conclusions. But as time went on, the process of analysis allowed me to accept what had happened to me and live with it without bad feelings.

One of the revelations was my insatiable desire to go into business on my own, to be my own boss.

Two years of intensive work passed. Our times together, and my times alone between sessions, were sometimes hurtful and upsetting, sometimes intriguing, but lately they had become pleasantly routine. I enjoyed having someone who knew everything about me on my side, supporting me unconditionally. This meant, I was to learn, that I was ready for the last phase of the psychoanalytic process: the "termination phase." I had to learn to let go and stand on my own two feet. Easier said than done, but I finally reached the end of the last session where I shook Dr. Morgenthaler's hand for the last time and said goodbye.

Psychoanalysis has changed me fundamentally and made me the person that I am today, no longer shy, full of self-doubt, and afraid of authorities. I did have contact with Dr. Morgenthaler several more times, but on a friendly basis, until he prematurely died at the age of sixty-five. My whole life, my behavior, my relationships, and my sense of self changed in a deep and abiding way. I was ready to conquer the world. And as a matter of fact, my final session with Dr. M was on the eve of my start-up of PickPay.

What I learned
from this experience

I The value of psychoanalysis.

Like no other experience in my life, psychoanalysis allowed me to disperse the dark clouds of my early years and bring my real self out into the sunlight. I am sure I would not have been as successful in my activities without it. Since then psychoanalysis has become much more sophisticated and has developed into a helping hand that can succeed in much less time.

2 To interpret my inner voice accurately.

I didn't like Dr. Morgenthaler at first and would not have gone back to him but for Dr. Brown's busy schedule. That would have been a loss for me. It was fundamental to my growth that I look inside to determine the origin of my antipathy to Dr. M. Now, whenever I have extremely strong emotions toward someone, positive or negative, I try to figure out why, and I often come to surprising conclusions.

3 The importance of dreams.

Dream analysis can be a critical key to accessing one's subconscious and suppressed emotions. But you have to be careful – it is not an exact science but a means of assessing one's emotions honestly. You have to guard against interpretations that give ground to wishful thinking.

Most valuable asset: employees

ONE of the biggest challenges faced by entrepreneurs is hanging onto qualified labor. I had a personal relationship with most of my employees. That was easy when our company was small, but even later, when we had hundreds on staff, I made it a point not only to greet them by name (something I learned from my mother at her restaurant) but also to be there for them when they had a problem. I experienced many interesting situations, but also, unfortunately, some sad ones, too. Here are a few of my most memorable experiences with employees.

Paul Richen

Paul was my most efficient store manager, working in that capacity at our second store in Zürich, which sold the biggest volume of all our stores. He was dedicated to his job and well liked by his customers, becoming an excellent role model for his co-workers. A good-looking man in his late thirties, with a full head of black hair, he was an all-round nice person. I always invited him to be a speaker in the seminars we organized for new staff members.

Paul's store was his castle. The only hobby he had was motorcycling in the high mountains in Switzerland. I didn't know much about his personal life. He was a private person, and in any case it was none of my business.

One day I noticed that he had lost a lot of weight. I was worried for him and told him not to work so hard. He hadn't taken a break for years and I sent him on a vacation so he could get back to his normal self. But when he came back two weeks later it was clear that something was wrong. He was even skinnier than before his vacation and became exhausted early in his shift. We sent him to a doctor for a complete check-up.

Shortly afterwards he spoke to me in private and told me reluctantly – which was so unlike him – that the doctor had just diagnosed him with AIDS. We didn't know much about that illness then, but there was a strong stigma attached to it. My doctor told us that there was no cure, that AIDS was a death sentence and he would go fast. I was devastated. It didn't matter so much that I was going to lose one of my best managers. I was shocked and distraught over the human tragedy unfolding before me.

I found out that Paul lived alone. He had no girlfriend, no partner, and no siblings. He was estranged from his parents. His only friends were his motorcycle buddies, and they didn't seem interested in his plight.

When he became too sick to work, we continued to pay him his full salary, and I visited him many times in his home. We had long talks in which, hiding my sadness as much as possible, I tried to help him accept the inevitable. On one of my visits, he handed me a sealed envelope bearing the inscription, "To be opened after my death – Paul Richen."

Paul died peacefully three months later. His letter stated that he wanted to be cremated and that I was to scatter his ashes on top of one of the Swiss mountains.

Lucie and I called his parents, and one warm Sunday afternoon we met them on top of Paul's favorite mountain pass, the Fluelapass near Davos. While the three others waited in a restaurant, I walked to the very top of the mountain, carrying the urn.

The weather was beautiful with absolutely no wind. The view was breathtaking. I said a prayer for Paul and then began to pour his ashes on the ground. But his ashes never touched the ground because at that very moment a gust of wind carried them away. This was a sign to me that he was resting in peace.

I went back to the restaurant, deep in thought. When the four of us sat down to eat something, I asked Paul's parents if they had had much contact with him recently. Even today, after so many years, his father's answer still shocks me.

"I haven't seen him since he was a thirteen-year-old boy," he said in an agitated voice.

I don't know what had happened between them, but Paul's father, even on a day like this, was still angry. I didn't need to hear any more. It was time for us to begin our descent home. A very sad but unforgettable day.

Mark Hains

By 1980, PickPay had grown to twelve stores and more than 200 employees. We began to experience problems. Mistakes and customer complaints were spiking, and so was shoplifting. I had always prided myself on my tolerant and motivational approach to my staff, but it seemed that some of them were now beginning to take advantage of me.

This was new to me and bothered me a lot. I just could not understand why some of my employees – and it was a small percentage of them, I kept reminding myself – had changed so much and why their motivation had suddenly dropped.

My wife and I discussed the situation at length and concluded that we needed better supervision and better control in the stores. We thought we could do that by hiring an inspector who would travel from store to store, unannounced. We wanted him to find out what was causing the mistakes and to help us figure out how to correct them. A headhunter suggested that I should have a look at Mark Hains, who was doing precisely this job for my main competitor, Denner. The headhunter suggested that I meet Mr. Hains.

Mark was a short, chubby man in his forties. He had short blond hair and very blue, penetrating eyes. I felt a bit ill at ease, even intimidated, when I met him. He certainly was authoritarian, but then wasn't that exactly what we were looking for? I put aside my doubts and hired him. He was let go immediately by my competitor and began working for us about a week later. I didn't have time to introduce him and asked Heidi, my secretary, to show him around, help him become familiar with the company, and introduce him to the store managers.

It didn't take long for things to change under our new inspection regime. There was a new atmosphere in the stores, which I thought was good – a sign, apparently, that Mark was doing a good job. I decided it was safe to concentrate on other things. I didn't have much choice. We had announced the opening of two new stores, located in Basel and St. Gallen, and I was frantically busy trying to make the opening deadline.

Heidi, who was very dedicated to our company, was a special person. She was bull-headed without being obnoxious, kind of tough in a friendly way, a strong personality with a soft heart. Here's just one example of the effect this unique combination of characteristics had on the company.

We were all heavy smokers, which was pretty common at that time. One morning I found an entry in my agenda, "Meeting with Paliwoda."

"Who is Paliwoda?" I asked Heidi later that day. She looked at me with a slight smile and said, "He is a famous hypnotist. Five of us are going there on Monday. We are undergoing hypnosis to stop smoking. And you are one of the five."

I did go – and it worked. I never touched another cigarette, in spite of having smoked a minimum of three packs a day. That is how Heidi was. Straightforward, direct, and always positive.

One day, after the new stores had opened, Heidi came into my office, sat down, looked me in the eye, and said, "You have to fire Mark Hains immediately. He is destroying the atmosphere with his intolerable attitude."

I was shocked to hear this about someone I had just hired, but when she briefed me on his performance, I was worried.

Mark was trying to establish a strict no-tolerance system in an open, tolerant, co-operative company. For instance, he would go into a store, run his finger over a shelf, and if there was dust on it, hold it under the nose of the store manager and tell him, "You call that clean? You are going to clean it right now and you are going to do it yourself!" And he would wait behind the manager until the job was done.

It was a clash of cultures, like asking a symphony orchestra to play a Sousa march, and I saw right away that I was responsible for the trouble. I let Mark go and reorganized the company by promoting some store managers to be team chiefs, with each one of them responsible for supervising five stores. That system worked well.

Paula Price

Paula was in her forties when she worked for us. She was very slender, about six feet tall, with just a touch of gray hair. She was an impressive personality. She worked at one of our checkouts and did a very professional job. As far as I knew, she was single and lived alone.

Paula worked with us for many years and became one of our top cashiers. But at one point I noticed a sudden change in her personality. She had lost some weight and was frequently absent from work or away from her register. Even when she was working, she wasn't as focused as she used to be. I asked her if she had a problem and whether I could be of any help. She said that everything was okay except she often felt very tired.

"Please go and see your doctor," I begged her. "Something must be wrong, and whatever it is, it is better to find it out as soon as possible."

She agreed and told me after undergoing a thorough physical that everything was fine. Her doctor gave her antibiotics for a bad cold, but that was it. She took a few days off and when she came back she was almost her normal self.

Something still didn't seem right but I couldn't put my finger on it. Time went by and Paula became very moody and unfocused. I had to take her off cash register duty and give her other work to do. I checked in with her regularly but she would not tell me what was bothering her. I finally gave up and even considered letting her go.

And then one day I got an urgent phone call from the manager of the store where Paula worked. Something very disturbing had happened and he asked me to come immediately. When I got to the store, he showed me a locker that he had opened because liquid was flowing out of it. He had found a bottle of vodka that had tipped over and broken, and another eight empty bottles. It was Paula Price's locker.

I confronted Paula immediately and she admitted that she had been an alcoholic for several years. She was addicted to vodka, stealing it from the store and drinking it in the bathroom. She must have stolen hundreds of bottles over the years. What amazes me to this day is the fact that no one ever suspected her. As I found out later, her visit to the doctor never took place. She had lied to me about that, too.

Although I felt sorry for her, I had to fire her on the spot. It was company policy that whoever was caught stealing was immediately let go.

A few days later, I contacted her again, but this time as a private person, not as her boss. I urged her to get control of her addiction and suggested that she join Alcoholics Anonymous. I believe she was successful in fighting her addiction, because several years later, probably as part of the AA process, she sent me a letter asking me to forgive her for what she had done. I wrote her back and told her not to worry about it. The matter was closed, I said, and I didn't hold it against her and wished her good luck.

What I learned
from this experience

1 It is never too late to settle differences.

I was shocked to learn how many years Paul Richen's parents had lost with their son. Instead of having a normal, loving relationship, there was nothing but anger. But I see many similarities with business. Sometimes things go wrong. That is the nature of the beast. But in most cases these problems can be mended, if one party makes the first step. Without this, the hurt or the misunderstanding or the war will go on and on, eventually hurting both parties. It is so unnecessary!

2 It is essential to train people to speak up.

It doesn't matter from what angle I view the Mark Hains story, I have to take the blame for it. I made the wrong decision at the wrong time. I hired the wrong person and didn't listen to my inner voice. And I didn't keep watch on his activities.

But making mistakes is common and nothing to worry about, if the mistakes can be, and are, corrected. But what did I really learn? I learned how important it is to have people around you that are not afraid to speak up. Heidi helped me correct my mistake before too much damage was done. I had asked her to always be direct with me and have the courage to contradict me.

3 Trust is better than suspicion.

It bothered me that I hadn't sleuthed out Paula Price's problem earlier. Admittedly, she was a master of disguise, but I should have seen what was going on. I guess I was still wet behind the ears. Even today, after my experience with her, I am not sure I would be any better at detecting similar situations. There is a fine line between believing in people and suspecting that they will do something negative. I am sure I paid much more than the cost of a hundred bottles of vodka for trusting people too much. But more often than not my trust was justified. I'll go with trust.

700,000
reasons to cry

KEEPING shoplifting and employee theft under control is a challenge that most retail businesses face. Not doing so can be deadly. In a food retail operation, for instance, margins are very, very small, and such losses can make them disappear altogether.

You cannot eliminate theft. In fact, you have to budget for it. At the same time, however, you must be set up a system to help you keep on top of losses. Realizing how important this was, I never delegated the supervision of inventory checks and controls, personally monitoring every store on a day-to-day basis. Whenever I saw losses even just approaching what was to be expected, I became actively involved, checking all the details vigorously and rigorously.

In our stores we used the Z-coupon system. At the end of the day, cashiers counted the money they had received during their shifts and typed it into their cash registers. The registers automatically issued a Z-coupon showing the difference between the cashiers' totals and the total registered by the registers. These coupons could not be manipulated. Each coupon was numbered and sealed inside the registers, inaccessible to anyone but the manufacturer.

As an additional monitoring method, we calculated the average purchase per customer and compared these calculations with our calculations for other stores in similar locations. We were always surprised and gratified to see how little variance there was.

About nine or ten years into PickPay, one store – the one located in Basel – came up totally out of line with the others. Its loss was so high that I knew there had to be more going on than shoplifting. Finding the cause became my highest priority.

I had built a small team of people I could trust. At the top were my wife, Lucie, who was in charge of double-checking the paperwork, and my chief supervisor and confidante, Tony Salmi, a man I trusted totally. Tony had been with us for many years, having worked his way up from stock boy to store manager to supervisor.

In the face of this problem, Tony and I decided our job was to closely supervise the store in question in order to catch the thief or thieves.

Shortly after our first meeting on the problem, Tony told us that he had discovered something. He said that one night when he was working late in that store, he heard a strange noise. Though he had no evidence to show us, he said he suspected that the tenants from the floor above had broken into the store and stolen merchandise. He said he also found several displays tipped over when he entered the store early one morning. We went to the police and they promised to monitor the building. That, however, turned up no clues, and the losses continued to mount.

Then Tony and I, unbeknownst to any of the employees, slept in the store on alternate nights for a whole week. Not the most pleasant experience, but it had to be done. Unfortunately, our sentry duty also provided no evidence.

I knew I was going to have to focus even more on this problem. But there was no way I could do that in my normal 24/7 work schedule. At that time, our yearly sales volume had just surpassed 100 million Swiss francs and we were opening new stores at a frantic pace. However, I was very fond of going for short breaks to our condominium in the mountains, sometimes as a working retreat, sometimes just to unwind from the weekly stresses. The condo was in Davos, a beautiful resort in the mountains, about an hour-and-a-half drive from Zürich, which was my hometown and the headquarters of my business. The peaceful environment of the Swiss Alps often helped me come up with ideas for marketing, strategies for developing the business, and solutions to the problems and challenges we were facing. In fact, these short stays had quickly become my preferred crisis-management tool.

This retreat was also where meditation first crossed my path. I remember the moment well. I was reading a book on the subject on one of these stays and was immediately fascinated. Practicing meditation on a regular basis from then on, I soon found that it increased my ability to understand problems and often pointed me to solutions that otherwise would have eluded me.

Gathering all the statements from the cash registers – hundreds of them – I headed for the mountains. Suspecting that the solution had to be somewhere in those papers, I laid them out one by one on the floor, on the table, on the bed. I walked up and down, picking up one statement, then another one, then another. But I could not find any irregularities.

Then I went for a long walk before continuing my painstaking search. Still nothing.

Finally I sat down to meditate, asking my subconscious to help me and show me what I was missing. After the meditation, or perhaps even during it, I fell asleep. I came to consciousness a few hours later and continued my search. But now something was different. I still picked up one statement after another, checking and double-checking them, but for some reason I kept returning to the papers that were lying on the kitchen table.

Then I saw it! One Z-coupon from April 14 had been altered. The change was so expertly done it was barely visible. Looking at it through a magnifying glass confirmed that an end number 9 had been changed into an 8. That could only mean that the original statement with the number 8 was missing. Someone must have manipulated one or several statements and pocketed the difference in the revenues. I knew I would probably find many more such manipulated Z-coupons. Case closed.

Or maybe not. Although I searched for a long time, I could not find any other manipulated coupons. By now my awareness was razor sharp. I had the feeling that I was pretty close to finding something.

The store had two checkouts and when I looked at the spreadsheet with the average purchase per customer, I noticed that one of the checkouts consistently had much lower numbers, for no apparent reason. How could that be? What caused the clients from this store to buy less at this register?

The answer hit me like a lightning bolt. I knew how it was being done and was sure who was behind it.

My descent from the mountains was matched by a greater and greater decline in my mood. I decided not to drive home but to go straight to the store in Basel, which doubled the length of my drive. By the time I reached the store, night had fallen and no one was there.

As I had suspected, I found, hidden in the storage room, an additional cash register. As I later found out, it was put at the front of the store in the morning and then at lunchtime replaced with the real register. The morning's revenues were taken from the fraudulent register and pocketed. Not even an unannounced inspection would have revealed the problem because the register in question was just like the others and was from our regular supplier.

There was only one person with the skill and the rank to pull this scam off and that was Tony. He must have used his authority as my right-hand man to order the register and have the bill for it directed to him. He must have paid the bill himself, with no one the wiser. I knew that he had to have had help from at least one other employee even just to move the register.

I hardly slept that night and the next morning went straight to the Basel police and reported my findings. They were very busy and when someone asked me if I was there to report an emergency, I said no, which fated to me wait for quite a while. Eventually I was called into a room. The officer in charge introduced himself as Paul Burger. He listened to my story, taking notes. He must have felt my anger and my disappointment and was trying to be sensitive in the way he asked his questions. I left all the evidence I had with him and told him where the third cash register was. He promised that the police would take action and get back to me later.

I left the police station deeply disturbed and headed off to visit another PickPay store in the city. When the cashier saw me, she asked, "Are you okay? You are so pale. What is wrong?" I told her I just had a headache and wanted to sit down in the office for a few minutes.

When she brought me coffee a little while later, she casually mentioned that Tony Salmi had given her an envelope to put into the safe, but as she did not have the code and the store manager was not working that day, she did not know what to do.

"Just give it to me," I said. "I'll take care of it."

As soon as she left the office, I opened the envelope. What a shock! I had in my hands proof positive that Tony had embezzled the business on a grand scale. It was a bank statement in Tony's name, showing a total of 700,000 francs, half a million U.S. dollars in today's currency. There were entries for almost every day of the year, each one for between a few hundred and several thousand francs.

I was relieved that the money was still there, but now the personal deception weighed even more heavily on me. I went back to the police, asked for Officer Burger, and showed him the bank statement. He said that they would bring Tony in for a confrontation. He asked me to wait and told me not to mention to Tony that I had found the statement.

As soon as Tony entered the room and saw me, he rushed over to me and began to cry.

"Please, please, help me," he said. "I am innocent. I didn't do anything. There must be a terrible mistake." Then he looked straight into my eyes and said, "Bruno, I am your friend. I could never do anything like this to you or PickPay. Please help me."

This last plea for help, from a man who knew he was guilty shattered any compassion I might have felt for my now former friend. I turned on my heel and left the station.

The police kept the bank statement as evidence for the trial. I later learned that Tony was found guilty on all charges. It turned out that he had been having an affair with the store manager and was accruing the money for her, not himself. However, because he co-operated with the investigation, provided evidence against his co-conspirators (the store manager and one other employee), and the money had been recovered, he did not have to serve time. Instead, he had to pay a fine and was put on probation. The bank statement remained with the authorities, to be returned to me when the case was closed.

About a year later, I would sell PickPay, remaining on the board for two more years to help with the transition of the business to the new owner. Shortly after I made the sale, the bank statement was returned to me. But the money did not come to me. It went to the new owner of the company. Even though I was still on the board of the company, there was nothing I could do about it. I had forgotten to put a clause into the selling contract that the money was owed to me personally.

The whole experience had given me 700,000 reasons to cry.

What I learned
from this experience

1 A clear distinction must be made between private and business issues.

This expensive mistake flowed from the fact that I let my personal feelings cloud my business perceptions, forgetting to put a clause in the contract, when I sold my company, that the 700,000 francs should be paid to me. I so wanted to put the incident behind me that I left everything to the lawyers. The lawyers did a good job, overall, but they were not responsible for my business interests. Ever since then, whenever something affects me deeply, I increase my vigilance concerning business issues as I deal with the personal issues.

2 Warning signs must be listened to, even if they are subtle.

This is equally important. My company grew so quickly that I neglected the warning signs. Looking back after it all happened, I wondered if there were any, and yes, there were. I remembered making an unexpected visit to the store one day and questioning why there was a third cash register. I simply accepted Tony's explanation that it was a repair unit. Whenever a bad and disturbing thing happens to you, be doubly careful not to forget the basics – trust your judgment and your gut instinct. You cannot delegate your responsibility. However, be aware that there is a fine line between being too trusting and being too suspicious.

3 The usefulness of meditation.

I can't recommend meditation enough. Going into a meditative mood has helped me many times to come up with the solution to a seemingly unsolvable case. I would like to encourage any entrepreneur or prospective entrepreneur to try meditation as a tool to find positive and ethically correct solutions that are harmonious with your personality. You'll find a guide to meditation in the appendix of this book, a guide I have written out of personal experence.

Goodbye,
PickPay

By 1982, I had been running PickPay for fourteen years. The company had become very successful. We had grown fast and did not owe any money to anyone. We now ran nineteen stores, took in revenues of more than 100 million Swiss francs per year, and were highly profitable. We could have expanded further. There was potential in the market and enough money and experienced staff members to make it happen. However, managing the business had become routine to me. Even new store openings, my favorite part of the job, didn't excite me anymore. Each one felt like the same experience in a slightly different color. I was still young and wanted to do something new and exciting.

And there was another problem. Managing such a big company was a 24/7 job leaving no room for private life. After fourteen years of this, my wife and I were tired. Tired of the tremendously long working hours, tired of the huge responsibility, and also a bit tired of the success. We were on the threshold of becoming a large company. One solution would have been to hire a general manager and let him run the business, but – and this was one of my limits as an entrepreneur – I just wouldn't have been comfortable with someone else running "my" company. Lucie and I had achieved more than we had ever anticipated. After long talks, we decided to sell. I must confess that I had to do a bit of persuading, but in the end it was a mutual decision, though not an easy one. The family relationship we had with most of our employees would be difficult to give up.

But it was not a simple matter. I wanted to determine the best price for our chain and, if possible, sell it quietly to the right firm, one that would keep the business going and keep the present employees in place. I was afraid that if the news of my willingness to sell got out, employees would begin to resign, competitors would take advantage of our transitional state, and our value would go down. Still, how was I going to find a buyer if I didn't put a for sale sign one way or another? I decided to try some behind-the-scenes maneuvers.

Michel Meyer, a tall, middle-aged sales rep, was a frequent visitor to our head office in the city of Zürich, which was located in the same building where we had opened our very first store many years ago. We occupied a whole floor, a few levels higher than the store Bauhof Zürich-Oerlikon, and this was where I had centralized the management, accounting, buying, and all related departments. We bought beauty products from Michael, and he always gave us a special deal. I had heard that he had a close connection to Karl Schweri, the sole owner of our fierce competitor, the Denner stores.

The next time Michel came in to sell, we had a nice chat. After the usual pleasantries, I told him that we hadn't made our final decision yet but that we were thinking about selling PickPay. I asked him to keep it confidential, which he promised he would.

A few days later, I received a phone call from Denner's owner, Karl Schweri. He said he would like to meet with me – for no special reason but just so we could get to know each other. It was kind of late in the game for that, I remember thinking. In all the years that we had been vigorous competitors, we had never met face to face. He certainly wasn't a friend and never would be. How could I forget the time he sent the police to our offices with a search warrant?

Of course I knew why he was calling, and I wanted to hear what he had to say. Because he also spent some weekends in the mountains, and in order to ensure privacy, I invited him to my condominium in Davos. When he rang the bell, I recognized him immediately. His face was familiar from the many profiles that had run in the newspaper. He was smaller than I had imagined, and was dressed in jeans and a gray sweater. His reputation as a fighter for many causes preceded him. He was politically active, a very intelligent, street-smart, and sometimes even ruthless man in getting what he wanted. Definitely a love-him-or-hate-him kind of guy.

"Welcome, Mr. Schweri," I said, inviting him in and pointing to the sitting area. "It is a pleasure to meet you for the first time."

Apparently he didn't believe in small talk. He sat down, looked at me with his trademark intense look, and, keeping an inquisitive eye on me, came straight to the point.

"I hear that you want to sell PickPay."

The directness of the question almost took my breath away, but I composed myself and said, "I don't think so, no. Where did you hear that?"

He just kept looking at me. I returned his look with a smile and said, "And I hear that you have just passed one billion in revenue for this year."

He looked surprised and said, "Where did you hear that?"

To this day I am proud of the answer I gave him. "You are repeating my question, Mr. Schweri," I said.

That settled it. We had sized each other up and now could get down to business. He really had just achieved that revenue mark a few days ago. He told me that the press release was scheduled for next week. I had made a wild guess and hit the jackpot, but I didn't tell him that.

When he repeated the question about selling PickPay, I again said no, but I also told him that we had no children and selling the chain might happen sometime, but not now.

"However," I said, "if we had an interesting offer, perhaps I could persuade my wife to make the move a bit earlier."

After a few minutes of friendly talk, his demeanor changed and there he was again, the sly and street-smart businessman. He stated a number and said, "And I will pay cash."

Now I was getting angry. The amount he mentioned was an insulting low-ball offer. I managed to hide my annoyance, however, getting up and thanking him for his visit, and wishing him good luck.

But now the word was out. It wasn't long before a large company in Germany got in touch expressing interest in buying PickPay. At about the same time I received a phone call from Beat Curti.

Beat was a well-known player in the highest social circles of Switzerland and a master networker. His family had been in the food-distribution business for generations and owned a wholesale company and several smaller retail chains. I immediately recognized that PickPay would be a valuable asset to him in his drive to become a food giant in the country. I had heard a lot about him, but we had never met.

We arranged to get together. For reasons of confidentiality, I invited him to our home. I looked forward to our encounter. It would be interesting to meet a person of his status.

Beat turned out to be an elegant, charming man in his mid-forties. He was a great conversationalist and an excellent listener with an impressive ability to focus his attention entirely on his interlocutor. He told me that he was interested in buying PickPay. He told me how impressed he was with the job we had done. He painted a vivid portrait of the powerful benefits that a merger would bring to all of us. He used all the right words, like promising to keep our employees and to continue PickPay on its present path. Last but not least, he offered a price that I considered a good starting point for a negotiation.

"Thank you for your nice words," I said. "I want to be fair and tell you that I already have an interesting offer from Germany. However, I would prefer to sell PickPay to a Swiss company. But I had another price in mind."

"And what would that be?"

Now I had to think fast. He meant business and so did I. I gave him a price that was above my expectations but that gave me some wiggle room. I was looking forward to further negotiations. But I was in for a surprise. Beat got up, extended his hand, and with a big smile said, "I agree."

So there we were shaking hands and sealing the deal. I couldn't help remembering the way my father did his cattle deals many years ago and was deeply touched by the situation.

While we were still standing and holding each other's hand, he said, "Let's make another commitment, to keep the price a secret. Is that okay?"

I agreed. When speculations about the size of the deal subsequently hit the press and went through the rumor mills, neither of us commented, and eventually the furor died down.

After the lawyers had done their paperwork and everything was signed, I stayed on the board of PickPay for another two years and then resigned. But that is not quite the end of the story.

Shortly after my resignation, Beat invited me to lunch at the Restaurant Kronenhalle in Zürich, a very special place, one of a kind. Founded in the 1800s, it grew to become Zürich's most famous restaurant. The cuisine is wonderful, but the real attractions are the original paintings on the wall by the likes of Giacometti, Picasso, Matisse, Miró, Chagall, Kandinsky, and others, just there and for everybody to enjoy. This stunning collection of masterworks was collected by the owner Gustav Zumsteg over a long period of time when these then-unknown artists painted them to pay for their meals. The value of these paintings today has been appraised at more than 20 million Swiss francs ($15 million US in today's currency).

When I came to the restaurant, Beat was already sitting at the table. I noticed a huge box standing beside him. Our mealtime conversation passed pleasantly. When dessert was ordered, he lifted the box onto the table and began opening it. This caused a lot of commotion and eventually everybody in the restaurant was looking at us.

Once the box was open, Beat said, "This is a gift for you that I hope will show you my appreciation for what you have done in helping us transform the company. Thank you very much and I hope that we will remain friends."

And out of the box came a beautiful oil painting by my favorite French painter, Roger Muhl, which Beat had commissioned to be made for me. It was a gorgeous flower scene. What a great surprise and what a wonderful gesture.

I never look at the painting without being flooded by warm memories of those times and of Beat Curti.

What I learned
from this experience

1 Timing is important.

There is a time to begin and a time to end. An entrepreneur has to be in the business with all his heart and soul. When he is no longer committed, he has to quit and find another challenge. It is dangerous if he doesn't. I have met many entrepreneurs who had an excellent and promising start but who, after a few years, when their entrepreneurial spirit was choked by routine, failed.

2 Entrepreneurs must know and accept themselves.

I could have stayed in the comfortable position as owner of a successful chain, but that wouldn't have been right for me. And I could have made more money by taking the company public, but that also wasn't me. The saying "it's lonely at the top" very much applied to me. We sometimes have to make decisions that are painful at the moment but beneficial in the long run. Shying away from those decisions may cost you dearly.

On the spot
with Microspot

WHILE negotiating the sale of PickPay, I began to think about what I was going to do next. I was only fifty-two years old, and my blood was still capable of being stirred by a new business venture. But what kind of venture?

I had always been interested in technology. My hobby, when I got to practice it, was short wave radio transmission. I am a licensed radio amateur with the call sign HB9BOB. Everything technical fascinates me – my friends call me a techno nerd.

At that time, personal computers were just hitting the market. Being a gadget junkie, I was knowledgable enough to see that they were going to revolutionize our private and business lives. Here was a business opportunity that was new and exciting, one that fit my personality and interests more than opening another discount food business.

And so after careful research I opened the first computer store in Switzerland, calling it Microspot. I leased a 1,000-square-foot store. It wasn't in the best location but it was still in downtown Zürich, close to many corporate offices.

Because I was not free of PickPay quite yet, I looked for a manager who could handle the new store for me. A friend recommended a man by the name of Max King. I interviewed him shortly thereafter, formed a good impression of him, and hired him on the spot.

When the negotiations for the sale of PickPay were done and all the papers signed, my wife and I escaped winter in Switzerland by going on a three-week vacation to Hawaii. We thought we deserved a little break before I got too heavily involved in the next venture. I gave Max the key and left.

It was a cold and windy night when we got home, but I was not interested in a quiet evening before the fireplace. I had to go to the new store and see how things were progressing. To my surprise, I found the shelves practically empty. Wow! Everything sold! That was wonderful. So my assessment about this new business opportunity was right. I applauded myself for my foresight.

However, on the drive back to our apartment, I began to feel some bad vibrations. I didn't sleep much that night, with all the excitement, jet lag, and nascent worries. The next morning, as soon as the bank was open, I called and asked for the balance of the account. The account was about where it was before I had left. No new deposits had been made.

The truth slowly emerged. Max had given computers to casual visitors to the store, allowing them to take them home to play or work with them. He failed to establish a paper trail – he didn't even know who these people were. Naturally, it was practically impossible to retrieve the merchandise now. Only a few honest types returned the computers or came back in to pay for them.

I talked to Max and asked him if he could think of any other names, but he couldn't. When I confronted him with the fact that he had almost bankrupted Microspot, he just didn't understand.

"They will bring them back," he said over and over again. "They promised to keep them just for a few days."

But they didn't bring them back, and I suspected that something gang-related was going on, but there was no way Max understood. What a bad judge of character I had been! I let him go.

My self-congratulatory applause quickly turned into self-castigating boos. Instead of being proud of my foresight and sitting back while the cash registers rang, I had to deal with a mismanaged store, dishonest customers, and a virtually bankrupt company. Here I was, the man who had just sold a successful business for an excellent price. The man with a good reputation as a retailer. What was I to do now?

The damage had been done. The easiest thing would have been to take no for an answer. I could have closed the store, paid for the damage, and wished my dream a sincere and relieved goodbye. But I didn't really even consider this a valid option.

To give myself time to think, I closed the store (I put a sign at the entrance, "Temporarily Closed for Renovation") and went for long solitary walks, reflecting on what happened, why it had happened, and what could be done. This helped me see things clearly. The truth was not easy to accept, especially because I was under a cloud of self-doubt, anger, and frustration.

I knew deep down that I was not going to give up the idea of developing a computer store, even if it had begun on a bad note. The basic fact, the business potential, had not changed. Computers still had a promising future. The only thing that had changed were my own feelings. I was hurt and angry that someone had taken advantage of me. My first reaction was to look for a scapegoat. How could my friend recommend such an unprofessional person as Max? How could Max give away expensive equipment without a paper trail?

However, the deeper my analysis and introspection, the more I knew I had to face the truth: that the whole fiasco was nobody's fault but my own. I had to take full responsibility for what happened. It was I and no one else who had acted unprofessionally. I had not done proper research before hiring Max. I had not supervised him. I was the only one who could have prevented the whole mess. Once I was able to accept reality, however painful it was to do so, I could let go of my frustration and begin focusing on the future.

I decided to give the store a second chance. After letting Max go, I put some of my own money into the bank account and took the closed sign down. Next, I rearranged the store, putting my desk in the very middle of the floor in order to serve customers better and have total control of everything that happened. I reopened the store, managing it myself from there on.

I practically had to start from zero, restocking the store, finding employees, and thinking about marketing. I did put a sign outside that read, "Now hiring, apply within." Then I had to become knowledgable in computer technology and find customers. It felt good to take things into my own hands, and it was fun, too. It was exciting to be involved on the retail and user side of this new technology.

In the midst of all the negative happenings around Microspot, I experienced a stroke of luck. On the very first day of the reopening, a woman entered the store, asked for the manager, and introduced herself as Antoinette Justus. She was a good-looking woman in her late thirties who exuded a positive attitude. Everything about her had the stamp of a winner: the way she talked and the way she immediately grasped which were the most important details. Antoinette turned out to be informed about computers. I hired her and never regretted it. She turned out to be a jewel. She was very knowledgable and was well liked by customers and employees alike. She played a big part in the successful turnaround of the company.

The store became a huge success and turned out to be my last hurrah in active business. A year after opening it, I was approached by a large company interested in buying it. I really was ready for a rest now. I sold it for a good price and was pleased to see that company go on to grow it into a multi-store chain. I, meanwhile, moved on to other things.

What I learned
from this experience

1 Searching for a scapegoat is a waste of time.

Without any doubt, the most important step in my solving this situation was deciding that searching for a scapegoat would be a waste of time – that the mess was of my own making. Once I accepted this, it became clear how I should solve the crisis.

2 The centrality of personal commitment to the task.

Making the decision to manage the store myself had personal consequences for my wife and me. After working exceptionally hard for many years and after having sold PickPay, we were looking forward to an easier life. Taking the reins like this was something I could do only because I was deeply dedicated to entrepreneurship. I already knew, by that time, that a dedication to working longer hours and being willing to sacrifice time and energy were what would make the difference between success and failure.

Once an Entrepreneur...

Part Four

Introduction

AFTER I sold my last business, I was still pretty frisky and ready for more adventures. When you're chronically wet behind the ears, you keep trying new things – witness the stories in this part about my ill-fated purchase of a farm in Arkansas; my decision to write books, in the process discovering that publishers were not lining up to sign me to their lists; and even my packing up and moving from Europe to Canada, in the process going from hero to zero, forced to start all over again.

But I'm not complaining. Not at all. Not when my little rebel and I have new adventures waiting for us every morning.

Moving on to new adventures

AFTER we had sold our companies, I was looking forward to a quiet life. I planned to travel the world and spend time with my hobbies that had been so neglected over the years I was in business. One of these was playing ping-pong. I joined a club and trained once a week and sometimes over the weekend, when we played tournaments. I enjoyed having the opportunity to meet some nice people, most of them much younger than I but all dedicated to Table Tennis, as it had to be called. ("Ping-pong" was considered to be a bit condescending, not appropriate for the professionals we wanted to be.)

I took TT seriously and even bought a proper table and a ball-server. The latter, positioned at the opposite end of the table, fired more than a hundred balls at me, its eager partner, alternating its speeds and using various angles. These athletic implements were housed in my basement, where I spent countless happy hours of practice. My regimen paid off. My game improved considerably and I placed better and better in tournaments. I was poised to become the darling of our club, which pleased me no end. After all, I had just passed my fiftieth birthday and most of my colleagues were in their twenties or early thirties.

From time to time we took weekend seminars, organized by coaches under an interesting setup. We played in a huge room that could accommodate maybe forty or fifty tables. In order to put the players into the right classes, the organizers tested our skill levels. The way they did this was very clever. You began playing at the table of your choice, with the exception of the three tables at the top, which had to remain empty until the actual game was under way. From time to time a referee would blow a whistle. The player at each table with the higher score at that moment moved up one table and the loser down one table. Then the playing continued. By the end of this, whoever finished at one of the top five tables was in the first group. Everyone else was in the second group.

I remember one such day in particular. I won most of the time that day, moving up the ranks steadily. At one point my adversary was a twelve-year-old boy. He was hardly taller than the table. I decided to let him win a few times so he wouldn't lose interest in the game. I got my comeuppance for my presumptuousness, however. This little guy was an outstanding player and he kept on winning. I think I have never underestimated anyone more. He was an exquisite player and a nice kid, but the latter quality did not stop him from giving me a proper caning. As soon as I saw my upcoming demise, I lost my focus, making his rout of me all the more dramatic. I even had the thought that my little opponent had turned the tables and was letting this nice old guy win a few points to keep him from feeling discouraged.

When the selection process was over, I ended up in the last category and finally had to acknowledge that I was too old to play with the twentysomethings and thirtysomethings . . . and the twelve-year-olds. It was a wake-up call for me.

I continued playing, but just for fun, moving on to my next hobby challenge: Citizen Band radio. At that time CB was much in vogue and I bought a license. The craze really began in 1977 with the movie *Smokey and the Bandit*. CB is a private two-way communication service, pretty much like cell phones today, but free and anonymous. You never used your own name and instead picked a call-name. I gave myself the name Parrot – some of the names of my conversation mates were Humpty Dumpy, Friendly, Cat's Meow, and Pumpkin, all fantasy names that would or would not reveal something of the identity of the speaker. I had interesting experiences flitting about the radio waves as Parrot. I met new people and made a lot of friends. Then it became known that CB attracted crime and that people were lured into secluded areas where they were robbed. I was disgusted that my favorite hobby had fallen prey to criminals and decided not to continue. Instead I moved up one step on the ladder, becoming a licensed HAM operator.

HAM operation was international and had no limits. But in order to get a license, I had to take classes and learn the techniques of worldwide communication. It was a long haul with several exams. I had to learn Morse Code, and this was a problem for me, not because it was difficult to learn but because my little rebel started acting up.

"You're not going to have any trouble on that exam. Take it easy," he told me.

Sometimes the little rebel came to my aid, but other times . . . Well, let's just say that I failed the test utterly. I was given another chance and from that day on Lucie trained me. It must have been boring for her to dictate word after word for hours every day, but she did it and I am very grateful to her. Three weeks later, I passed with flying colors, got the full international license, and was assigned the call sign HB9BOB.

That was when the fun really began. I immediately had contact all over the world, could point my antenna in any direction, and over time talked to people in more than ninety countries. It was a wonderful hobby and, as I have always been a techno junkie, the many sides of HAM operation fascinated me.

But something was missing. I just wasn't ready yet for a life as a hobbyist and needed another challenge. I realized that an entrepreneur can't just let go of his passion for playing a part in the business world. Once an entrepreneur, always an entrepreneur.

Over the years I had become knowledgable in money matters and had helped many of my friends with money-management advice. I also took seminars. The way money flows and its effects were always fascinating to me.

In a case of perfect timing, the editor of *Sonntags-Zeitung*, the largest Sunday paper in Switzerland, called me. He wanted to know whether I would be interested in writing a weekly column. Readers would ask me questions about money matters. I was excited – it would be great to write for a newspaper. Being able to express my thoughts in writing had always intrigued me but to this point I had no time to practice this passion. I told the editor the column would certainly be interesting, but that I would have to know more before deciding.

And so I did some research into the financial problems that members of the public were falling into. What I found out shocked me. Many people had lost their retirement nest eggs because they had believed the sweet-sounding voices of the scammers and invested their money dangerously. Neither the government nor the banks were doing enough to warn the public, and there was no strong voice to inform about these dangerous money gambles. I decided to get involved. I accepted the newspaper's invitation and began a weekly column that we called "Dear Mr. Gideon."

What began as a small idea became a full-time job. I was pleased to be able to help people and warn the public against shaky investments and give them sound advice on how to invest their money. It was the first such column in Switzerland and it became an instant success. In a matter of weeks we were snowed under by hundreds of letters, and I personally answered each and every one of them. I could have answered only the questions that were interesting enough to be published, but that wouldn't have been fair to the readers.

The job fascinated me and the editor gave me total freedom,

which meant my little rebel had no reason to complain. Not only did I answer letters, I often tried to recover money that was mismanaged by banks and other institutions for the people asking my help.

I had a stroke of luck when I met Otto Helbling, a nice, sociable, middle-aged man. He worked as money manager at UBS, the largest Swiss bank. He agreed to meet with me once a week to look through the letters from readers that were too complicated for me to answer. Otto was very knowledgable. He was a true professional. Even the most complex questions were no problem for him. I met him every Wednesday at his office at the bank. Otto was invaluable. I was always very outspoken in my column, and he often warned me about the consequences. I am sure he prevented me from being involved in some ugly lawsuits. And on top of this, he was a great personality and our collaboration was the beginning of a great friendship that is still going strong today.

I was always well received at banks when I had to approach them. But carrying the "calling card" of a powerful newspaper made it much easier to get in touch with them and to defend my readers' interests.

I vividly remember a letter that I received from a woman, Paula Noty, who lived in a rural area, high up in the Swiss mountains. She apparently wasn't very sophisticated. Her letter was worded very strangely and bristled with typos. Paula wrote that she had inherited 100,000 Swiss francs (about $80,000 U.S. in today's currency) from a deceased uncle. She had given the money to a bank to manage, whereupon the money manager had lost it all. What could she do?

I felt sorry for the poor woman. Losing so much money must have been a terrible shock and must have had a big impact on her life. I decided to look into the situation and asked her to send me all the documents. They arrived in an envelope with so many errors in the address that it was sheer chance that they reached me at all. Otto and I spent a lot of time researching the case and we eventually found out that the money manager had indeed made some inexcusable mistakes and had mismanaged Paula's money.

I contacted the bank and explained the situation. They double-checked my findings. After much discussion, they realized that I would not let go of this poor defenseless woman's case and finally agreed to reimburse the money.

An ugly case that I remember was one involving a father, who wrote:

Recently I received a phone call from the tax department. The caller identified himself as Mel Smith. He apologized for a mistake they had made and that they had calculated my tax bill too high. In order to return the money, they would need my account number and, as identification, the password. I gave him the information and he even congratulated me for getting money back. The money never came, but my account was emptied to the last drop. What can I do?

I knew immediately that there nothing could be done. The bank's reply would be, "This problem is clearly his fault. To give the account number and the password to an unknown person is more than careless." But I decided to look into the situation anyway. I called the man and asked him to explain the situation again. I could not see any reason that he should be reimbursed. I told him that I was very sorry but there was nothing I could do for him.

This poor man's case was not an isolated one, unfortunately. I was stunned to see how many people believed others good-naturedly and followed their "orders" without thinking. I had to keep repeating my advice, "If it is too good to be true, it is!"

And then, after working for this newspaper for about three years, the *Beobachter*, Switzerland's largest paper, with more than a million readers, asked me to join them, and I continued my "Dear Mr. Gideon" column there. *Beobachter* means "Observer" in

English. Its mission statement is to defend the interests of less fortunate people, something that was close to my personal beliefs.

I was also invited to give seminars and public speeches to readers of the newspaper. I greatly enjoyed the direct contact and interaction with people.

I felt very comfortable in that environment, but of course the huge circulation of the paper substantially increased the number of letters received and added to my workload. But for the first time as a journalist I had an infrastructure to help me in answering them. It was still a tremendous job, however, and even with the help of my secretary, Gisela, there was no end in sight. I worked almost day and night, but the letters kept coming, until eventually it became unmanageable.

As time passed, I realized that I was on the verge of becoming a "celebrity." Newspapers began referring to me in a kind way as the Money Uncle, a nickname that stuck with me later when I was invited to take part in a TV series called *Netto*, which only added to my name recognition. People recognized me on the street and some of them asked questions about their money problems point blank. I didn't like this part of my "retirement" and began to look for another way to write.

And so after six years and a total of about 20,000 letters answered, I decided to pass the pen to someone else. It was a difficult decision, as I had tremendously enjoyed my job. My last speech was scheduled as a goodbye appearance, and I was surprised that more than 700 people attended. After I had delivered my speech and voiced my warning against scammers once again, I received a standing ovation, a wonderful concluding note to this part of my life.

And that's when books came into view. I enjoyed the process of writing. I was fascinated that I could turn a blank piece of paper, or an empty computer screen, into a meaningful piece just by my creativity and my ability to put thoughts on paper. Now I was going to do so on a bigger scale.

What I learned
from this experience

1 Staying grounded protects entrepreneurs from big mistakes.

If you are an entrepreneur at heart, chances are that you will be very successful. With this comes the fact that you will be well recognized and will suddenly find many new "friends." That's when the danger begins. You will have to make a decision between the hard work of an entrepreneur and the sweet life of socializing and partying. If you decide for the latter, and even if you call it networking, this could be the beginning of your downfall. I know of one entrepreneur, a friend of mine, who at the height of his career began to delegate the accounting of his company without supervising it. When he realized that things were going terribly wrong, it was too late. And there was no one there to help him. His new "friends" had disappeared.

2 You can never be too careful.

My newspaper column allowed me to advise the public against scams. Where money is concerned, ethics often disappear. The same advice should be given to entrepreneurs. People in business, investors, even family and friends will be attracted to you because of your success. They will float ideas past you. Take them with a grain of salt. My advice to my readers, "If it is too good to be true, it is!" is as valid with respect to business as it is to private life.

3 There is a time to begin and a time to end.

I have been a new entrepreneur many times and have always felt that there was a time to end a venture and find something new to do. Maybe it is my inner drive to explore new things, maybe it is my zodiac sign (Gemini), or maybe it's just my nature or my little rebel, but I have learned that in situations that are too complicated, too difficult to manage, or even just too boring, it is time to move on. And the best way to do so is to make a clear break, whenever possible without hurting others. In the case of the money column, I quit only after they had found a successor, just as in selling PickPay I had chosen a buyer who would take care of my employees.

A new challenge: writing books

WHEN my work at the newspaper ended, I decided to write a book. I was looking forward to an exciting time of putting my thoughts and my experiences into a real book. So far all I had written was op-ed columns and articles for newspapers and magazines and some short stories for my own enjoyment. After long deliberation, I decided to write about the difficulty many people experience when confronted with a no and methods they could follow to change it to a yes.

I had been interested in this topic my whole life. It was an issue that came up repeatedly in my columns. I was always amazed that most people accepted a no even with regard to problems that could be easily solved. Most people, when they received a no from a bank or some other authority, just accepted it and didn't dare to dispute it. Why? Because a no is a rejection and that is sometimes difficult to handle.

As can be seen in many stories in this book, it has always been my hobby to find a way around a no and to turn it into a yes.

However, book writing proved to be more challenging than I expected. Getting from an idea to the finished product was not as simple as I thought. I wanted to get across that not accepting no for an answer – while not becoming aggressive about it – was one of the most important qualities of an entrepreneur. It was important for me not to just write a book but to present this idea in a way that would help others to learn how to fight a rejection.

It took me six months to write the book. Then followed another six months in which my manuscript was put through the normal hoops that books go through: editing, cover design, typesetting, printing, and shipping. The book was an instant success and in a short time my publisher sold more than 50,000 copies. I was hooked. I decided to continue writing books.

I remember one day I put my notebook and some snacks and water into my backpack and hiked up to a forest in the mountains. There I found total peace and could concentrate on my writing. I called it a writing picnic. It was a sunny day and I was at peace with the world. I was inspired by my beautiful surroundings and just kept working away.

I was so absorbed in the theme of my writing that I completely forgot the world around me, until I sensed some uncomfortable warmth and heard some strange noises. I looked behind me and was horrified to see that the forest was on fire and that I was right on the edge of it. There was just enough time to get myself out of the danger zone before trees began crashing down and the fire began to run wild. I headed as quickly as I could to the first human settlement, but the fire brigade was already on its way up. The whole forest burned down; there was not much the firefighters could do. I later learned that some picnickers had unintentionally set the forest on fire.

I went up to the same mountain twice after that. The first time was just a few weeks after the fire. It was devastating to see that what was once a beautiful landscape was now black, smelly, and dead. I returned about two years later. Amid the black trunks of trees I saw that new growth was going on, already visible in some places. That reminded me that nature also doesn't take no for an answer.

All this gave me food for thought. Is a writer a different species of person than an entrepreneur? I came to see that, all things considered, every artist, writer, painter, songwriter, musician, or actor is a self-employed entrepreneur. The criteria that make for a successful entrepreneur apply to them as well. Even if their artistic activities are their passion, they will eventually have to sell their products or their production or their talent to make a living.

And in order to do that, just like any entrepreneur, they will need to catch people's attention. They will have to make sure that people want to buy what they produce or show. And that means they will have to promote their art and will have to network and seek public and media attention.

I didn't realize all this when I started writing. I thought it was just another hobby. But I soon found out that, like many things in life, it wasn't as easy as it looked. Writing is a lonely job, because writing is only part of the job. Most of the time is spent in rewriting, rewriting again, and again and again. You can only be successful if you have a deep passion for words and the effect of those words on others. My problem was that I was used to being in contact with people all the time. Sitting by myself putting words into my computer was very different. I needed people to talk to in order to determine whether my thoughts and views would stand up to their criticism. I needed people in order to come up with ideas and associations that wouldn't occur to me on my own. I also needed people to help me get over writer's block, a common problem in every writer's life.

But how could I find such people? Most people shy away from criticizing anyone even remotely artistic. But not my wife, Lucie. She was very straightforward in her responses. She knew her own mind and voiced her opinion honestly and in a way that I could accept. That was exactly what I needed.

And there was someone else: Martin Brugger. I met Martin at a book launch and was immediately fascinated by him. He was fiftysomething, an impressive personality not only because of his appearance – he was more than six feet tall – but also because of his communication skills and deep love of books. Whenever he talked about books – and that was pretty much all the time – he had fire in his eyes. Martin was general manager of Oesch Publishing, a company with a great reputation in the book world, one that specialized in self-help books. Oesch had excellent contacts with the other German-speaking countries. When I asked Martin if he was interested in publishing my books, he immediately accepted and we became business partners.

Martin was compassionate and at the same time critical. I haven't met many people with this unusual combination of characteristics. He had a very pleasant way of telling me that a piece I had written could and should be improved. He did so by telling me it was not up to my standards and I should consider rewriting it. And he also told me how to do so. I valued his input and our casual acquaintance soon developed into a mutual friendship that is still very much alive today.

I took my new career seriously and continued writing. In my next book, *Not at My Expense*, I dared to write about another theme that was close to my heart but that was not as closely related to the business world. I needed to do a lot of research first.

I was always interested in psychology and could never understand why many kind and good-natured people are treated poorly by their spouses or colleagues. It so happened that I had a few examples among my closer friends. I came up with the theory of the "kick-me sign," which is what I call the learned experiences that take place at a very young age and that are deeply implanted. I dedicated most of the book to the solution of these problems. *Not at My Expense* was also an immediate success and I received a lot of feedback from readers.

The third book, bearing the title *The Gideon Principle*, was about balance in life. I strongly believe that life is like a walk on a tightrope, where it is vitally important to be in perfect balance. If we are not, we are at serious risk.

I have written seven books in German, of which two so far have been translated into English (*Don't Take No for an Answer!* and *Not at My Expense*). The book you are reading right now is the first that I wrote originally in English. I also write a weekly commentary in English, the *1 Minute eMail*, which goes out through the Internet to more than 20,000 subscribers.

The reason that I have always enjoyed writing, this difficult, lonely, emotional, and always entrepreneurial job, is twofold. First, it has allowed me to systematize the knowledge I learned in business while still wet behind the ears. Second, it has given me a vehicle for giving back to the business community and the public in general the benefits of my experiences, good and bad.

What I learned
from this experience

1 The entrepreneurial requirements of writing and publishing.

Writing is one thing. Publishing a book is an entirely different matter. Most writers write their book and the rest is done by the publisher – if they are lucky enough to find one. But if you don't find a publisher – and that happens to most of us writers – you either have to self-publish or forget about it. But you can be successful in self-publishing if you act as an entrepreneur. That happened to me when I moved to Canada, as I will describe in a later story, and that experience allowed me to see both sides of publishing more clearly.

2 The importance of finding a critic.

Writing is a lonely job and finding a critic allows you to see your topic from another angle. It is vitally important for anybody involved in the art of writing to find someone who who will critique their work honestly, openly, and on a regular basis – not necessarily to change what has been written, but to broaden the horizons of the writer. In the case of this book, it was not only my editor who told me openly when I needed to rewrite sections or when something was not clear, but also many of my friends who took the trouble to read the manuscript and give me suggestions for improvements.

3 The danger of delusions of grandeur.

Writer–entrepreneurs must be careful to avoid the trap of developing delusions of grandeur. As a successful writer, you will have many invitations to speak and to appear on TV and radio. This may build you up as an important personality. There is nothing wrong with that, and if you enjoy being the center of attention, more power to you. But the danger is that you will begin to live in a world different from the one in which you wrote your masterpiece, and the writing of your next book is likely suffer for it. Just remember, your fame is not permanent. It will fade away as soon as another star rises.

I nearly bought
the farm

AFTER I sold my companies – and during my time as "Money Uncle" – I had acquired some knowledge of the complex question of managing money. I have always been a very cautious investor. I diversify my funds and make sure rebalance my portfolio every quarter. But managing my own money isn't something I enjoy very much. I find it boring to deal with figures instead of people, so I let professional money managers do the job for me.

My accountant in particular kept telling me that my normal practices were not enough. I needed to invest some money outside Switzerland. It was the time of the Cold War and one of his favorite expressions was, "Better safe than sorry!" He talked about hard assets, long-term investments, growing value in land, and not putting all my eggs in one basket. What he said made sense, and after some research I decided to buy a farm in the United States. At that time it was fashionable to invest in the land of the free and the home of the brave.

I knew a lot about retailing, about marketing, about growing a company, but absolutely nothing about farming in a foreign country. How do you go about buying a farm in the US? A "friend of a friend" introduced me to a real estate agent who specialized in farmland there. Over the course of several telephone conversations, this agent, Ian Benson, told me what a great investment this would be and how much money other clients of his had made investing in farmland.

Eventually my wife and I flew to meet him in Memphis, Tennessee. Ian, a friendly man in his forties, was going to show us some farms. I thought we would drive to see them but instead we flew over the countryside in his private plane. I was impressed! I had never been in a private plane and it was quite an experience, frightening and exciting at the same time. I found it electrifying to fly over farms and think that I could own some of that land.

But I wanted to do some proper research. I made my headquarters at the Peabody Hotel in Memphis, a remarkable town in itself with interesting places to visit, such as the Elvis Presley home, Graceland, Beale Street, and the Zoo. But what made the stay even more special were the hotel's five ducks, who came down from their quarters every morning at exactly eleven a.m. They used the elevator and then swaggered proudly through the main hall to their fountain in full view of the public. At five p.m. they went back the same way, often to the applause of onlookers.

But I wasn't there to watch birds showing off; I was there to do some research on buying a farm. So back to work. I met several real estate agents, looked at different farms, and finally decided on a farm in Twist, Arkansas, less than an hour south of Memphis. It was a beautiful farm, all flat land, 99% tillable, and way out in the country. They grew milo and soybeans and had several ponds for catfish. I had my U.S. lawyer, Philip Andis, look at the property to make an assessment, and he saw no reason not to proceed.

When the day had come to sign the deed, I went to Philip's office to finalize the transaction. What happened there I will never forget. We met the seller, a shy and extremely overweight man – he needed two chairs to sit on – and his lawyer. While my lawyer's secretary finished the paperwork, we heard a commotion outside the office. Philip went to investigate and was surprised to see the Sheriff, who carried a summons to be delivered to Bruno Gideon once the deed was signed and not before. I had no idea what this was about. I headed over to talk to him, but my lawyer took matters in his own hands and told him that nothing was signed yet and would he please wait outside.

Coming back to our meeting, Philip said, "Trust me, I believe I know what is happening. When the deed is signed, you just go out the back door and my secretary will drive you back to Memphis. As that is in another state, the Sheriff cannot deliver papers there and you will be safe."

"Safe from what?" I answered heatedly. "I have nothing to fear and he can deliver whatever papers he wants."

But Philip said, "Believe me; I know what I am doing. You go to Memphis. Not having these papers delivered to you will save you a lot of needless trouble."

I was baffled. What did I have to do with the U.S. court system? I had no idea why court documents were being delivered to me. But I decided to follow my lawyer's advice. As soon as the papers were signed, I said goodbye and left through the back door, to be driven back to the Peabody in Memphis. The next day I flew back to Switzerland.

A few weeks later the papers were delivered by diplomatic courier. The situation became clear to me. A broker in Boston, a person completely unknown to me, had taken legal action against me for not having paid his commission. He was suing me for a huge amount. That didn't make sense at first, but when I called Philip and read the papers to him, he explained it to me.

"First of all, in this country," he said, "the seller has to pay the commission, not the buyer. So the whole lawsuit is bogus anyway, but I have done some research and can tell you why they did it. Many foreigners buy land in the U.S. with undeclared money and they don't want it to become public. So lawyers routinely search for foreigners who are buying land and then sue them. Because the foreigners don't want any trouble, they pay a ransom to have the lawsuit dropped. Their information system must be excellent."

"As far as I am concerned," I answered, "they can sue me for anything they want. I don't have any undeclared money at all. But what is going to happen now?"

"I am not a clairvoyant, but I am pretty sure that they will call you and offer to drop the lawsuit if you pay them money."

He was right. About two weeks later, I received a phone call from Boston. It was the lawyer for the plaintiff, who chatted with me as if nothing had happened. He told me how much he liked skiing in Switzerland. He said he was sorry we couldn't meet on a nicer occasion but he was acting purely on behalf of his client.

"I told my client not to go ahead," he said, "but you know how some clients are nowadays. They never listen to their lawyers – well, we will just have to deal with that . . ."

On and on he went until I interrupted him. "But how can you sue me for something that is absolutely not true? I have never even heard of the man in Boston. What you are doing is not fair. Shouldn't you double-check the information before you involve innocent people?" I was angry but tried to keep my voice calm.

"Well, you have a point there," he said smoothly, "but it is too late now. You will have to deal with court problems. You will have to hire lawyers in two countries, and that could go on for a long time. The Swiss authorities will also be informed. There will be huge costs for you to fight this. But let me talk to my client and I'll get back to you."

Two days later, he called again. "I spoke to my client and he told me that he would be ready to drop the case if you would pay him his expenses, and that would be the amount of $120,000 U.S. Think about it and let me know."

With that he gave me his number, wished me a great day, and hung up the phone.

I called my lawyer and told him about the discussion. He wanted me to send him a written report, which I did. I also told him that I would *never* pay anything, not even a penny, to these scammers. I added that I wanted to mount a countersuit but only to protect myself, not to take revenge. I never heard back from the Bostonians but later found out that they tried the same scam on others. I believe that my lawyer tried to disbar the other lawyer, but I don't know whether he succeeded. For me the matter was closed. I was ready to enjoy my farm in Arkansas.

But it turned out that it wasn't the enjoyment that I had envisioned. I experienced all the problems of an absentee owner: cheating by employees because of lack of supervision; embezzlement; and non-performance of duties. The first farm manager I hired passed my background check as squeaky clean. People told me that he was very experienced and trustworthy. But it turned out that he couldn't resist the temptation of defrauding someone when there was little risk of discovery.

I did discover what he was up to and replaced him with another manager, whereupon history repeated itself. After four years I realized that the farm was too much of a hassle and disappointment and I decided to sell it.

I had to take a substantial loss. When I went to Memphis to sign the sales documents over to the new owner, who was an American citizen, he must have thought I had a massive tic or was a certified paranoiac. All through our meeting, I kept looking over my shoulder expecting to see the Sheriff.

Did it bother me that I had to take a loss? To be honest, yes, it did. But it was my own fault for going into a business in which I was a complete novice without proper preparation. But there was a blessing in disguise. Shortly after I sold the farm, the dollar began a steep descent and today it is worth only one-third of what it was when I changed my U.S. money back into Swiss francs.

What I learned
from this experience

1 The importance of sticking to one's knitting.

Retail entrepreneurs, however successful they become, are in a way "local successes." They start with what may know, whom they know, how their business works, and how to apply that knowledge to daily situations. Although they have open minds and are interested in many other things and even have a well-developed ability to hear the grass grow, they develop business smarts through working with known entities. When financial advisers get them outside that comfort zone, bad things can happen.

2 The importance of personal supervision.

Entrepreneurs, or anyone for that matter, should never make substantial investments in anything they cannot supervise personally or through a totally trusted person. The risk of corruption is too great and so is the temptation. And that is another point: it is an entrepreneur's responsibility not to create a situation in which it is too easy for people to do unethical things.

3 Scams will always happen.

My lawyer told me that I should sue the plaintiff and his lawyer. I understood him – that he was coming from the other side and had to make a living. But I decided not to. It would have been an act of revenge without any positive outcome. On the contrary. I would have had to invest a lot of time, energy, and money for no good reason. People will always try to make money from stupid people and I just wasn't stupid enough for them. They got the message, so what good would it have been to go after them?

Never too late
to learn

BEFORE my farm experience, another investment in the U.S. turned sour on me but that time I was able to put my entrepreneurial experience into action very quickly as soon as I caught wind of what was happening.

"Want to be a winner? Invest in real estate!" Jack Sonic used that pitch again and again. He had lots of impressive examples to support his statement. Such as a client of his who had doubled his money in six months.

I was experienced enough not to fall for this kind of verbal advertising. I had come to the United States from Switzerland to find investments and had been introduced to this man, a "money-hunter" who worked for different companies trying to find financing for them. I took an instant dislike to him and his way of bragging. He was a particularly unpleasant example of a pushy salesman.

While I was determined to have nothing to do with him, I did follow up on a lead he gave me and contacted the owner of READ, or Real Estate Advanced Development, a small company in Florida. The owner's name was Bobby Fells, a balding, bespectacled man in his forties. He had a hands-on, craftsman look to him. We met at his home – I never saw his office – and he explained his business to me. READ specialized in remodeling kitchens and rooms in houses that were going up for sale so that the owners could get more for them. The whole concept made sense to me, but I wanted to see some numbers.

"Certainly," Bobby replied. "I was expecting you to ask. We are very proud of our numbers. I'll have my secretary, Cindy, contact you about this."

The next day his secretary came to my hotel. She introduced herself as Cindy Palm and gave me a folder of papers from READ's accountant.

I liked Cindy from the very beginning. She was about five feet, four inches and had a wonderful personality. She was very pleasant and friendly and you couldn't help but feel good in her company. I invited her to lunch and we chatted about this and that. She was just a messenger from READ, so I didn't ask her any questions. Before we parted, I asked for her home address and promised to send her some Swiss chocolate as soon as I was back home in Switzerland. That was the beginning of a good friendship that has lasted for years.

The paperwork looked good and I decided to give READ an interest-paying loan. We agreed that I would also get a percentage of their profit. I invested $50,000 first, and then another $50,000 later. From time to time they sent me reports – all of them excellent – from their accountant and I felt I didn't need to worry about my investment, all the more so because they always paid the interest on time.

One day Cindy called me collect. It was about five in the morning and I figured she wasn't aware of the time difference. She told me that she was no longer working for READ. Her salary hadn't been paid for the last three weeks and she had an offer for an interesting job that she had accepted. She gave me her new phone number and told me that she hoped to stay in contact with me.

"You haven't been paid for three weeks?" I asked her. "How is that possible? Did you have a falling out, or is there a problem with READ that I should know about?"

Cindy didn't want to say anything about this at first, but when I insisted, she told me confidentially that she had another reason for leaving. She was just tired of all the phone calls from collection agencies and having to explain again and again that they would be paid soon.

I thanked her for her confidence, but what she told me set off alarm bells. I asked her to try to get more information and told her that I would see her soon. I took the first available plane and flew to Florida. Before I even contacted the company, I met with Cindy. She had been able to dig up more information and told me that Bobby had invested my money as a down payment for a house in Palm Beach for himself and his friend Martin.

"I believe that READ will soon go out of business," she said. "It would have been over for the company a long time ago if it wasn't for Martin, Bobby's friend and partner. Martin trades on the stock market and has very deep pockets. He helped Bobby, but that can't go on forever. One day he will have to stop the flow of money into the company."

That was very bad news indeed. I thought for a long time about how I could get my money back. I contacted Bobby and told him that I was in the U.S. and wanted to meet him and Martin on a personal, private, and urgent matter. We met the same day, again at their home. I was careful never to smile, displaying a depressed attitude.

"Thanks for having time for me at such short notice," I said. "I am not here to talk about READ – I know from your accountant's reports that it is doing well."

Then I turned to Martin. "However," I said, "I have a personal problem and need your help. I have made some bad investments and am short of cash. I am asking you to agree to repay my loan right away. I will agree to take seventy-five percent of it but sign off on the whole amount, which means that you won't owe me anything afterwards."

They looked at each other, and before Bobby could speak, Martin agreed and right there wrote a check for $75,000. He had me sign a rapidly drafted release of my loan and the interest to that very day.

I thanked them, wished them luck, and immediately went to the bank to deposit the check. It was good.

A month later, READ declared bankruptcy. I would have lost the loan completely if I had not acted. It was only fair that I give Cindy a substantial thank-you present. After all, she helped save me from losing a lot of money.

What I learned
from this experience

1 Research is the key to preventing bad investments.

It was a major mistake to let Bobby manipulate me into closing the deal at his home, instead of meeting with me at READ's office. If I had had a chance to look around their office (if there was one at all), I might have suspected their motives. But the most serious mistake I made was believing what they told me without talking to some of their clients and their accountant. Even though I lost some money, and was lucky in the end, the deal would never have happened in the first place if I had conducted proper research. Conclusion: never make an investment on the spur of the moment; always double-check the facts first.

2 Honest information comes from people lower on the totem pole.

Had I not established such a good connection with Cindy, I wouldn't have had her input. I didn't befriend her with this in mind, but the situation showed me that the best, most reliable, and truest information about what's really going on in a company comes from the people at the base of the company, because they know the daily realities and are in constant contact with clients.

3 Being an absentee owner poses a double risk.

As I later learned, the paperwork from the accountant was fake and so was the whole organization. If you are an absentee owner, every direct investment you make has a double risk – the normal risk that any investment has and an additional one that comes from not being able to supervise the operation yourself. This means you have to be doubly careful with such investment opportunities.

Still wet
behind the ears

By now, the mid-1990s, I had reached the age at which most of my peers were putting on their slippers, throwing another log on the fire, sipping some hot Swiss chocolate, and sitting back to read the paper from stem to stern. I had already lived two or three lifetimes in my business years, so the prospect of slowing down like this was tempting. I tried it, but I just couldn't do it. As always, I was easily bored, and it certainly wasn't in my nature as an entrepreneur to sit back and dream (unless it was about starting another business).

In my travels I had been to Toronto, Canada, many times and had fallen in love with the city and the country. Everything there – the wide open spaces, beautiful scenery, remarkably tolerant people in a society with strong protections for minorities, and a low crime rate – was so different from what I was used to. The city was lively and lovely. What impressed me most was how it was informally divided into several multicultural parts, such as Little Italy, Chinatown, Greek Town, the Jewish area, and so on. Toronto was a striking cross between a North American and a European city. I was amazed by how well these cultures mixed.

From the first time I set foot there, I experienced a warm coming-home feeling, and the more I saw it, the more I liked it. When my personal situation changed, I decided to move to Toronto and became a permanent resident (a "landed immigrant") of the country.

It was quite a change for me. At home in Switzerland, many people knew me from my business successes, public appearances, my newspaper column, the TV show, my books. Over time I had built a network that gave me immediate access to lawyers or doctors or any other dignitaries. I knew most of the players personally. And very often strangers approached me on the street just to ask me questions relating to my work as "Money Uncle."

But in Toronto I was just one of many. I had no special privileges. It was as if I was starting a new life on another planet at age sixty plus. However, I treated the task of finding my way in this new environment as yet another challenge. Bring it on, was my attitude. Be careful what you ask for – you might get it!

One of the first things I needed was a credit card. After filling out the application, the bank gave me a ridiculous limit of $1,500. After standing in line, I asked the teller for a higher limit. He looked something up on his computer screen and told me in a flat tone, "This is the maximum for you. You have no credit history." Without even saying goodbye, he turned away and actually said, "Next please."

That roused my little rebel, who egged me on in no uncertain terms. I turned back to the teller and said, so everyone could hear, "Some courtesy to a customer would be appreciated." He didn't even look up, acting as if he hadn't heard me and repeating, "Next please." I was definitely not in Switzerland anymore, Toto.

In a country as big as Canada, you need a car and a driver's license. My Swiss driver's license was not valid here. Instead of contacting the Swiss consulate for information, I followed my little rebel's goading. I had to do it right away; it couldn't wait. I went to driving school, took the lessons, and passed the test. Less than a week after that, I was informed that a mutual agreement had been reached between Canada and Switzerland with the result that a Swiss driver's license could be exchanged for a Canadian one without a test.

Hard-won driver's license in hand, I proceeded, logically, to buy a car. I picked the model and negotiated the price. Everything went well. Two weeks later, when I went to pick up the car, I wrote a check for the whole amount, signing it and handing it to the car salesman. To my dismay, he refused to take it.

"We can only accept a certified check from you," he said.

"But why?" I asked, feeling like a criminal. "My check is good. Go ahead and call the bank, if you doubt it! And what do you mean by 'from you'?"

His answer was something I would hear many more times in my adopted country: "Sorry, it's just company policy." And he added a sentence that was also becoming familiar to me: "You have no credit history."

Needless to say, he lost the sale and I bought a car from another dealer.

I didn't foresee any problems with my English, until one day, after having been in the country for only a few weeks, an exchange changed my mind.

During a pedicure treatment, the pedicurist said to me casually, "I see that you have athlete's foot."

Considering this a compliment, and pleased that my daily workout was yielding such positive results, I replied, "How nice of you to say that. Thank you very much."

The poor lady looked up at me and broke into roaring laughter. I didn't know what was so funny. Finally, when she had regained her composure, she told me what athlete's foot really was.

The message was loud and clear. I had to improve my English. I proceeded take classes and attend discussion groups.

This sharpened my conversation skills and also helped me to make a rough translation of the most successful of my books published in German, *Don't Take No for an Answer!* I wanted to publish it in English and release it to bookstores in North America. So I wrote a proposal and sent it to several Canadian publishing houses, but my efforts were met with total disinterest. They didn't even give me the courtesy of a reply. No matter how I attempted to contact them, whether by e-mail, phone, or even letters, all I got in return was silence. They flatly refused to talk to me.

Those rejections stung, all the more so because I knew that the book was good. After all, I had sold more than 50,000 copies in German-speaking Europe. Two publishers eventually returned the manuscript, but only after many, many interventions on my part. They hadn't read it. I knew this because the small slips of paper I had put into it were at exactly the same places when I got the manuscript back.

But they didn't ignore me because they were unfriendly, rude people. They were bombarded daily with loads of manuscripts and they couldn't read all of them. Their primary impulse was to reject, unless something special or the name of the author caught their attention. Guilty until proven innocent was their working principle. Nobody knew who I was, I had no name recognition, I was a total stranger. The proverb, "It is not so much what you know as whom you know" was being proven yet again. How different from life in my native country! Now I was no longer a hero – I was a zero.

No, I would not accept that. I was more determined than ever to bring my book to the public.

One day I got a phone call from Patrick Crean, the editor of a well-known publishing house. He had read my manuscript and wanted to talk about it. He invited me for lunch to a Japanese restaurant. This gave me new hope. Patrick was in his early fifties, about five feet nine inches. His most impressive feature was an intense but at the same time kind and gentle look. He grasped immediately what I was saying. He asked the right questions and listened carefully. He had read my manuscript, liked it, and told me that he would recommend it to his boss. And he took a lot of time to explain how the publishing business in Canada works. When I was later informed that his company would not publish my book because it didn't fit their line, I wasn't really disappointed. Just the fact that someone had complimented me on my work and believed in me helped keep me going.

And then, out of the blue, Peter Urs Bender called me. He said that he, too, was Swiss. He had heard about me and asked if he could be of any help. A few days later I met Peter, a middle-aged, good-looking, and high-energy man who always had a nice smile on his face. We found out that we had lot in common and amazingly similar experiences in our early years in Switzerland. Peter was a well-known professional speaker and book writer. On top of that, he was also a very nice person. It was a pleasure to exchange ideas with him. He always had time for me and became actively engaged in helping me, introducing me to people who might be important for my career. I learned a lot from him.

It was a very sad day, years later, when he called me and told me in his honest and straightforward way that he had been diagnosed with cancer and that he had only a short time to live. There wasn't a trace of self-pity in the way he said it. And then came the amazing, but for Peter quite typical, question: "Is there anything I can do to help you while I am still around?"

I tried very hard to blend in to his casual talk, but I was deeply touched. From then on, it was time for me to pay him back. He lived in Stratford, about an hour and a half from Toronto, but I visited him on a weekly basis, called him often, and tried to keep his spirits up. Until one day I learned that he had passed away. I had lost one of the best of the many good friends I had made in my new country.

But life goes on and the next step had nothing to do with publishing my books. I had invited some friends for dinner, over which we discussed life in general. The discussion became heated when some of the guests exchanged their ideas about a topic that

I had raised: "What is the most important thing for anyone to achieve in life?"

Sheila, a successful money manager from a local bank, vehemently defended her opinion that making money was the most important goal, because it gave you everything: recognition, respect, and the power to buy anything you wanted. I was opposed to this view but didn't have a chance to voice it because Tony, a manager and active politician, cut in, arguing that the attainment of power was just as important.

"Our life has an expiration date," he said with emphasis, "and we have to use the time we have to get into a power position. He who has money and power always wins – it is as simple as that."

I was diametrically opposed to their views and after a while spoke up, trying to bring my point into the discussion. Being the host, I had to be gentle.

"I agree that your points are important," I said, "but in my opinion they are not the most important and don't work because they are egocentric. We live in a society that can only survive when giving and taking is in balance. Why don't you mention anything about giving to others, about paying society back for your good fortune?

"And there is another point," I said. "Your idol is winning all the time. You are in a permanent battle to make more money, to get more power. But sometimes you are going to lose – and of course you know that. When that happens you will have to learn to let go – something you won't be able to do if you are totally focused on making money and getting more and more power."

I paused to give someone else a chance to speak, but everyone remained silent. So I continued, "Of course you have a right to live the life that is right for you but I believe that you are on an ego trip and sooner or later you will have to pay for the fact that you're not giving to others."

Then I said, "I have a final point that I think is vitally important, but I don't want to dominate the discussion."

Again, a receptive silence.

"The final point," I continued, "is about accepting criticism – no, I want to correct myself – about actively *seeking* criticism. This is one of the most important points, in my opinion, because it ensures that you are always grounded. I have met too many people in my life who exercised their power, didn't accept criticism, and weren't grounded anymore, living in a world of their own making. Inevitably, they went under."

Shortly afterwards, everybody said goodbye. The next day Sheila called me and asked if I would write down my philosophy so she could forward it to her friends. She didn't have to persuade me to do this because we were talking about my favorite subject. I wrote separate e-mails about each point and even gave my cyber-missives a name, the *1 Minute eMail*, because I wanted them to be short and to the point.

That was the beginning of something new, unique, and very surprising, because the audience for my jottings grew at an unbelievable speed. I created the weekly *1Minute eMail* at my own expense and I sent it out absolutely free. More and more people showed interest. Within two years, more than 20,000 people from all over the world, all strangers to me, had subscribed. This effort is a source of great satisfaction to me. I am pleased to receive feedback from subscribers and to learn that I have been able to change the lives of some people a tiny little bit. One thing that helped its phenomenal growth was listing it on a motivational speakers' and writers' website, but other than that, the service grew based on the entrepreneur's best friend: word of mouth. Satisfied customers are always the best marketing plan.

But let's get back to the book. A writer with the desire to bring his book to market but who can't find a publisher has a choice. He can surrender and bury his dream, or he can self-publish. If he decides to do the latter, he will need to hire many professionals: an editor, proofreaders, and a designer, not to mention a printer, publicist, and distributor, and all this before his book is ready for the bookstores – all in all, a long, complicated, and cumbersome process.

Surrender was not an option for me. Being an entrepreneur at heart, I wanted to conquer my feeling of isolation and rejection. I decided to establish my own publishing company, which I named Matterhorn Publishing Inc., a small Canadian company domiciled in Toronto. I was in business again and a new entrepreneurial cycle was beginning.

But I needed someone on the inside to tell me how that business worked and to open doors for me. That person turned out to be the man who would become my mentor and editor, Don Bastian.

It doesn't happen often, when you get to know a person, that you get the feeling that this new relationship has the potential to develop into something special. This happened when I met Don. He is the very image of the bespectacled editor. He has a quiet self-assurance and a gentle demeanor with no rough edges to be found in his personality. It is a pleasure and delight to communicate with him. Don had been an editor for a big publishing house and had just begun a new freelance business, thus making the transition himself from employee to entrepreneur. I later learned that I was one of his first clients, and only after we had worked together for a few weeks did I learn that he was one of Canada's top non-fiction editors. I was not surprised. What at first was just a job developed into a friendship between us and our families.

Don is the person who helped me more than anyone else in getting a foothold in Canada, and I am very grateful to him. He told me that I should now write in English, which I did for the first time with this book, and he helped me navigate the shark-infested waters of book publishing. Eventually my book *Don't Take No for an Answer!* was printed, distributed, and on the bookstore shelves. And I immediately began writing this book.

At this time my application to become a Canadian citizen was approved and the citizenship department invited me to a swearing-in ceremony. Some friends came to witness the ceremony, which took place at eleven a.m. It was a very touching event. When it was over, my friends invited me to lunch to celebrate my new Canadian citizenship. After the lunch one of them, Dan, suggested that we drive out of town to look at an interesting property, but there was so much traffic on the highway that we turned around and drove to the lakefront for a long walk. It was after four when we drove back into our neighborhood.

When we got out of the car, what did I see but forty of our friends, all dressed in red and white, standing on the terrace, waving at me and singing the national anthem. I was so overwhelmed with this unexpected gesture of welcome, friendship, and love that I started crying and couldn't stop for a long time. To me it was no coincidence that red and white are also the national colors of Switzerland. I took it as a sign that the transition was successfully completed. I was home.

The Seven
Essential
Lessons of
Entrepreneurship

THE fact that you are reading this book tells me that you would like to be an entrepreneur or may have already launched yourself into that grand experience. Either way, my advice is go ahead, do it, or keep on keeping on. But be sure to learn from the mistakes of others, on the one hand, and from their successes, on the other.

Speaking of which, I have boiled down all of this book's "what I learned from this experience" sections into the Seven Essential Lessons of Entrepreurship. To speak in entrepreurial terms, these lessons are the bottom line of the bottom line of the bottom line in running your own business. Here is the list, which is followed with some elaboration.

1	**Believe in yourself**	**5**	**Manage conflicts**
2	**Be committed**	**6**	**Welcome criticism**
3	**Stay in charge**	**7**	**Don't get too comfortable**
4	**Be flexible**		

I
Believe in yourself

> Magic is believing in yourself. If you can do that,
> you can make anything happen.
> — Johann Wolfgang von Goethe

What do I mean by believing in yourself?

If you have a realistic idea for a new business or product or endeavor of some kind, don't be afraid of failure. Listen to your inner voice. If it is strong enough, *go ahead and just do it.* Don't give up and don't let Caspar Milquetoasts or naysayers talk you out of it or distract you from achieving your goal. You are the only one who can fulfill your dream. You are the boss. You decide.

What is the risk in this?

The risk is bound up in the first words of the paragraph above: "If you have a realistic idea . . ." In being careful to avoid naysayers, you could fall prey to "yeasayers." In fact, one of the greatest skills you must develop as an entrepreneur is the ability to discern intent and value in everything that is said to you.

You have to ask yourself, "Are the people who are cheering me on just trying to be nice? Are they biased because they hope to benefit from my success? Do they have experience and knowledge to back up what they're saying?"

But you also have to ask yourself questions regarding the people around you who are urging caution. For example, "Are they trying to slow me down because of their knowledge or because they are cowardly or wish me not to succeed?"

So listen carefully, discern intent, and never forget that the final decision is yours.

What is the reward?

If you believe in yourself and have circumvented all the obstacles, you can pat yourself on the back and be proud of your decision. You will be successful and there is no doubt that this will improve your self-confidence. But there is more. Your accomplishment will be a role model for others in similar situations and that is something you can be proud of.

Here's an example of Lesson 1

A friend of mine, through intensive networking, signed up for the rights to set up McDonald's franchises for the whole of Switzerland. He decided to open the first one in Basel. He secured a good location and began his preparations for the opening.

McDonald's was not well known in Europe at that time, so he consulted friends about the validity of the franchise. Most of them discouraged him from going ahead. It was too American – Europeans wouldn't respond well to fast food, they said. He could lose his shirt extending himself with a business deal that covered a whole country. Raising capital would be almost impossible.

The result? My friend was spooked by all the arguments. Against his convictions, he withdrew. McDonald's found another franchisor, and . . . well, you can imagine how successful it is in Switzerland by now.

2
Be committed

> Unless commitment is made, there are
> only promises and hopes . . . but no plans.
> — Peter Drucker

What do I mean by being committed?

Your new venture will be a 24/7 job, at least during the start-up phase. Life as you know it will change totally. You will have to be committed to working harder, will enjoy less free time, and will experience new challenges. To sum up: you will practically have to give up your private life, and for a good long time. Ask yourself, "Am I willing to do that?" If you are not, forget becoming an entrepreneur.

Is there a risk in this?

Definitely. Make sure that your wife or husband or partner "signs on" to your new venture. The personal transformation you're about to experience will have ramifications for them. If they decide to work with you as a team, that would be the best solution. If that is not possible, for whatever reason, and you have to go it alone, make sure that the temporary stress you will experience in the first phase of your venture will not cause problems for them. And try to get their emotional support.

What is the reward?

Success as an entrepreneur. Being committed the way I'm talking about is an indispensable condition and a sure-fire recipe for success – and for stronger self-confidence.

Here's an example of Lesson 2

Evelyn worked in the travel business for many years and always dreamed of going into business for herself. But she didn't know how. She also struggled with her weight and could never find clothes that would fit her full-figured body. She watched her weight go up and down with the latest diet and would find herself with a closet full of clothes that didn't fit anymore.

Then she suddenly had the idea of pitching the target market of overweight women and opened a store that she called What's Mine Is Yours. Women who lost weight could exchange their clothes there and the same thing went for those who gained weight. Evelyn gave up a secure job and steady paycheck to make her dream come true.

Not surprisingly, she was very successful. Her commitment was born out of her own need, which made that commitment all the stronger.

3
Stay in charge

> When you take charge of your life, there is
> no longer need to ask permission of other people
> or society at large. When you ask permission,
> you give someone veto power over your life.
> — Geoffrey F. Abert

What do I mean by staying in charge?

As your company grows, you will have to delegate and that could open a can of worms. Be very careful when you pass on responsibility, especially where money is concerned. At all times keep ultimate control. You *always* have to keep on top and you can do so only if you control the benchmark data.

There are many examples in this book showing the damages I sustained when I delegated without enough control. See "On the Spot with Microspot." And don't forget Alois Job, who gave me a lot of freedom but emphasized that I was to report to him weekly. See "The First Cash and Carry."

Is there a risk in this?

Absolutely. The risk is that you could end up exercising too much control, which would demotivate your employees and unnecessarily add to your workload because of an increased need to solve conflicts. There is a fine line between too much and too little control. Both are wrong.

What is the reward?

The reward is that you keep control of your operations and your company stays alive. Giving up control can be deadly for your company, as the following examples demonstrate.

Here's an example of Lesson 3

I know a successful entrepreneur, let's call him Mr. X. Toward the end of his fiscal year, his general manager told him that everything was going well and that they would realize a net profit of $22 million. That was all that Mr. X wanted to hear. No questions, no cross-checking, no queries as to details. When the year-end accounting was done, a loss of $18 million was revealed. The company had to be sold at a fraction of its value. Mr. X went out of business.

And here is another one

Barings Bank was Britain's oldest and financially strongest merchant bank. It was so old and prominent that it had even financed the Napoleonic wars and the Louisiana Purchase. Barings was also the bank of the Queen of England.

In 1995, to the total surprise of the management, the bank collapsed and within one day went into bankruptcy. It turned out that one of their traders in their Singapore office, Nick Leeson, had made huge futures trades for the bank and the trades had gone sour. The sheer size of the transactions should have rung very loud alarm bells but no one within Barings' senior management seemed to notice any risk and the danger went undetected. The bank collapsed with lightning speed in February 1995, and Leeson was sentenced to six-and-a-half years.

4
Be flexible

Although I am flexible and ready to
take advice, I can't carry an umbrella of
thoughts over my head that would
distract me and affect my music making.
— Zubin Mehta

What do I mean by being flexible?

Just as flexibility is important for the health of your body, so it is
important for the health of your business. If you are flexible in
your business, you can make changes easily, which is yet another
factor that will help you stay ahead of your competition. Keep
your eyes open and anticipate trends. The market is always
moving. Looking ahead in this way is a major survival tool.

Is there a risk in this?

Yes – being *too* flexible, as you will see in the example below.

What is the reward?

Being able to change quickly – in response to market trends, for
instance – is a big asset. It will allow you to act early and not be overwhelmed by changes. And it will make your life more interesting.

Here's an example of Lesson 4

I usually shop at the same store for my clothes. Now this store has a new manager, who has the disconcerting habit of changing the layout of the store almost every day. I used to enjoy walking along the shirt shelves but now the trousers are there. And where they had trousers they now have underwear. And tomorrow it will change again. As a customer I enjoy knowing where everything is in "my store." But because of the absurd lengths to which this manager has taken the virtue of flexibility, I feel that it is my store no more.

5
Manage conflicts

Conflicts are inevitable,
but combat is optional.
— Max Lucado

What do I mean by managing conflicts?

Conflicts are a necessary evil in business environments. There is no business without them. Learn to accept and master conflicts and understand their importance. Don't take them personally even if they are meant to be personal. Don't think of taking revenge or getting even – that would be a loss of time and energy. Just deal with them factually and move on to your next challenge.

Is there a risk in this?

The risk is getting too involved in personal fights, which will distract you from focusing on your core business. A conflict can be an ideal opportunity for clearing the air. But that is possible only if you bring the conflict out into the open and vocalize it. The greatest danger lies in hidden conflicts.

What is the reward?

When the air is cleared, energy is freed up for more positive undertakings. Getting to the bottom of conflicts allows you to find out what is on people's secret agendas. But in order to do that, you will have to wait until you are detached from the issue. And to do that, you will have to learn to let go of the conflict.

Here's an example of Lesson 5

At the beginning of my book career, I hired a renowned publicist to market one of my books. He was expensive – very expensive indeed. But I thought it would be worth it in terms of book sales. His first bill came and I paid it. Then along came the second bill. I hadn't received any information about promotion and sales and I wanted to know what he had done so far for my book.

Answer: nothing, nothing at all. He had given the job to one of his employees who was "still thinking about it." I told him that I wasn't going to work with him any longer (which must have been a blow to his ego) and that I wouldn't pay the second bill. He said that he would get back to me. A few days later I got an e-mail from him with only one sentence in it: "He who knows Bruno Gideon is not surprised!" I actually laughed at his intended insult and was glad that he had revealed his true personality.

6
Welcome criticism

Don't abuse your friends and
expect them to consider it criticism.
— Ed Howe

What do I mean by welcoming criticism?

There is a danger that sooner or later catches up with every entrepreneur: thinking inside the box. Being an entrepreneur can be a
lonely job, especially when you have to make important decisions
alone. Surround yourself with good people and make it a rule to
always keep your door open. Invite friends, family, business colleagues, clients, and professionals to give you their take on this or
that problem. If you do this right, you will get a lot of interesting
feedback, which will help you make fewer mistakes and keep
abreast of your competition. See "My Board of Critics."

Is there a risk in this?

You should look for feedback only on issues where you are unsure
of what to do or on broad questions such as, "Where will our
company be in five years?" or, "What are our weaknesses and

strengths?" Don't get too specific with your questions. After all, you don't want to have too many cooks in the kitchen.

What is the reward?

You will make fewer mistakes and will gain an advantage over many of your competitors because you can now think outside the box. This will allow you to open your mind to new ideas and anticipate new trends and that will help you keep a step ahead of your competition and grow your market share. Not many can do that.

And here is an additional thought: If you can find an ally, an experienced mentor, or a coach to help you, particularly in the start-up phase, go for it and listen to them! They will bring valuable insight to your enterprise and help you tremendously.

Here's an example of Lesson 6

Robert, a member of my family, ran a restaurant and wasn't very successful. As a matter of fact, he wasn't successful at all. When he asked me to help him I agreed and went to meet him. The location of his restaurant was excellent and so was its name. I suggested some changes to the front of the store and a marketing campaign, together with flyers to be distributed in the neighborhood. I told him that I would pay for the flyers, just to help him, but that he should approve the text.

And that is where the problems started. Unable to make a decision himself, he asked his customers, his friends, and people on the street and changed the wording of the flyer again and again. When I told him that I had a deadline at the printers and that I needed the final text by the end of the week, he could not deliver.

Robert was incapable of making a decision. When I confronted him with this fact, he got angry and shut me out. He couldn't take criticism and eventually lost his restaurant.

7
Don't get too comfortable

Eternal vigilance is the price of liberty.
— John Philpot Curran

What do I mean by getting too comfortable?

I have no doubt that you will be successful if you have what it takes to be an entrepreneur and follow the advice in this book. But remember, there are different stages in the life of an entrepreneur and each one requires different approaches, skills, and commitments.

First comes the all-consuming start-up phase – the breakthrough – requiring extreme tenacity, stamina, and independence of mind.

The second stage is one of expansion, requiring organizational and management skills. In this stage, you won't be able to do everything yourself and will have to rely on employees.

The third phase is when you have made it and the company can run without your being there all the time. This is when danger really kicks in. Don't forget how many companies have fallen when their owners were enjoying their success and partying rather than working. Even just a momentary lack of vigilance can send a company crashing to the ground. Beware delusions of grandeur.

Is there a risk in this?

There doesn't have to be. Let's say you reach phase three and you are not the type to enjoy arm's-length success. Then sell your company and start something new. The same is true at stage two for those who would rather start a business than manage it. In both cases, knowing your boundaries, listening to your inner voice, and staying true to yourself as an entrepreneur will help you through.

What is the reward?

Simply said: peace of mind.

Here's an example of Lesson 7

See above – this whole book!

Appendix

Meditation as a life and business tool

MEDITATION can be practiced anywhere, anytime. It is the best method I know for strengthening self-confidence.

There is no right or wrong way to meditate. The only rule is to do what works for you. Therefore, most of the questions listed below allow for several answers. The answers I offer simply reflect my own experience.

An important point in meditation – if not the key point – is breathing. Breathing is made up of three actions: inhaling, retention, and exhaling. An Indian text teaches that when we inhale, we take in universal energy (the future). When we hold our breath, we gather this energy (the present). And when we exhale, we release the spent air (the past). I like this theory, because it also teaches us to let go – of our anxieties for the future, our obsession with the present, and our chains to the past.

Meditation is a technique of concentration.

One form of meditation is mantra meditation, in which you focus on a phrase or an object – for example, a candle, a shadow, a light, or a spot on the wall. Whenever your thoughts begin to wander, they need to be led back gently to what you are focusing on.

Another form is association meditation. In this form, you reflect on a particular thought, a person, a problem, a symbol, or an idea (for example, God is love). In other words, you meditate on something specific – perhaps a problem you are dealing with at the moment.

Meditation can become an essential tool for you. Following are my answers to the most important questions I have been asked on this subject.

What is meditation?

The exact definition is controlled thinking. My personal definition is that it is all of the following: a way to the inner self; a prayer; and a means to achieve balance, obtain answers, find peace, and reflect on oneself. Another very different, but still accurate, way to describe meditation is as an anti-stress method without side effects.

What does controlled thinking mean?

When meditating, we try not to think about anything, thereby becoming open to hearing our own "inner language." This takes a lot of practice, because our minds like nothing more than to divert our attention. It is relatively easy to learn the technique of not thinking of anything, however. We can concentrate on our breathing and let our thoughts pass by like clouds. Thinking of nothing has a welcome side effect, one that millions of people have experienced as a common result of meditating: a greater ability to concentrate and a stronger memory.

Are there any rules to meditating? Is there a required meditation posture?

There are no rules. It is important only that you feel comfortable. You can meditate standing, sitting on a chair or couch or on the floor, sitting cross-legged (lotus position), lying, kneeling – whatever suits you.

What are the types of meditation?

There are two types of meditation:

- Quiet meditation, which does not seek concrete answers.
- Focused meditation, which concentrates on an issue you want to deal with.

Would you explain this further?

Quiet meditation is more popular. It is about listening to your inner voice. Focused meditation tries to find answers to certain issues. The technique is the same as that used in quiet meditation, but you are meditating on an issue. It is advantageous to summarize the issue into only one sentence (a mantra), repeating it quietly several times at the beginning of the meditation period.

How long should I meditate?

That is irrelevant. What is important is that you meditate daily. It is up to you whether you meditate for two minutes or two hours. Once you have developed a taste for meditation, you will look forward to meditating, most likely, fifteen to thirty minutes a day.

What will I gain from meditation?

A lot. You will be more composed and react more deliberately. You will be able to let go, look at your problems from another perspective, and be at peace inside, thereby gaining in self-confidence. Meditation will also help you achieve personal balance.

My personal approach to meditation

Over the years, as I have grown older and gained more experience and worldly wisdom (perhaps becoming a little drier behind the ears), my practice of meditation has changed significantly. This is not unusual. Meditation is a flexible process. Over time, if practiced regularly, it will develop into something very personal. In my case, through this particular approach to meditation, I have found a way to focus on many of my priorities, both professional and personal.

I would like to share this personal practice with you, but please accept it as a suggestion only. Don't feel any pressure to meditate in this fashion. It is possible, however, that learning about my approach may help you find your personal form of meditation.

I meditate in two phases. In the first phase, I go through the seven chakras, silently asking myself questions and answering them as honestly as possible. In the second, I meditate as described above.

First, let me explain what chakras are.

According to Eastern and Western philosophies, a chakra is a point of energy in our bodies. Though they are not measurable by any known scientific instrument, they are believed to be the source of balance and health. There are seven chakras and each one is associated with various factors, such as emotions, desires, thoughts, power, and health.

Now let me explain each chakra's location in the body and function, before going on to "talk to them" in meditation. You may skip this part if you like, but reading it will help you understand the method better.

The first chakra is the **Root Chakra**. It is located in the perineum, at the bottom of the spine, and represents one's grounding, fears, and self-doubts.

The second is the **Sacral Chakra**. It is located in the abdomen – more precisely in the genitals – and represents sexuality, survival skills, emotions, and desires.

The third is the **Solar Plexus**, located in the diaphragm and representing willpower and self-definition.

The fourth is the **Heart Chakra**, representing love, relationships, and self-acceptance.

The fifth is the **Throat Chakra**, representing communication and self-expression.

The sixth is the **Third Eye**. It is located between the eyebrows and represents one's intuition, imagination, and connection to the universe.

The seventh is the **Crown Chakra**. It is located at the top of the head — in the cerebral cortex of the brain. It represents one's awareness and connection to God, or to a higher power.

Here is how I include the chakras in my meditation.

The first thing I do is relax by belly-breathing for a few minutes. Then I concentrate my thoughts on the first chakra, the Root Chakra, and while doing so I ask myself a few questions related to what this chakra represents. For instance, I may ask, "Am I still grounded?" or, if I have just experienced a major achievement, "Am I still humble?" Whatever answers come to my mind I take seriously. I may or may not get answers right away but that is immaterial. The important point is that my questions trigger a thought process that will continue even after the meditation is over.

Then I move on to the Sacral Chakra and follow the same procedure. The questions here may be, "Am I in any way jeopardizing my survival?" or "Am I being responsible in my sexuality?" The questions could deal with whatever else is on my mind but they must be related to what this chakra represents. I may receive a lot of input here or none at all. Either way, that is okay.

Meditating on the Solar Plexus may influence me to consider such controversial questions as, "Am I about to cave in on something that means a lot to me?" or "Have I imposed my will on someone?" I usually receive a lot of input on this one and can often prevent problems by addressing these issues after my meditation is over.

Meditating on the Heart Chakra may provoke such questions as, "How can I improve my relationships?" or "Did I accurately express my feelings to someone?" Or I may even ask so basic a question as, "Do I love myself?" This may seem out of place, but it is not. Giving to others is important. But giving to yourself is just as important.

The Throat Chakra has to do with communication. The questions I ask myself are, "Have I offended someone by anything I have said?" This question is followed, of course, with, "How can I correct that?" This part of my meditation may also lead to corrective actions, whether immediately or a few days or weeks later.

When I get to the sixth chakra, the Third Eye, I ask, "Is the Universe or my subconscious mind trying to tell me something?" I receive amazing answers to this question. Just inviting your subconscious to "speak up" can be very interesting.

And finally, the Crown Chakra. Meditating on this chakra leads to the most essential questions, such as, "How is my relationship with God?" or "Do I want to change my spiritual relationship?" This part of meditation allows me to come to terms with my association with God. The way people meditate on this chakra will, of course, be very different from person to person, whether they are very religious or agnostic or even atheistic. Remember, you meditate for yourself. Your basic beliefs are nobody's business but your own.

Once I have proceeded through seven chakras, I continue meditating in the way I described at the beginning of this discussion. At the end of meditation, I just relax for a few minutes and then get up. If I fall asleep during or after meditation, that is okay, too, because the subconscious mind also works during sleep.

One more thought. Whatever the answers turn out to be, I am always very honest about them. Honesty is very important and not really that difficult, because what I am thinking and expressing is only between me and me. No one will ever learn of my thoughts or secrets unless I decide to share them. At the end of the meditation and for hours thereafter, I sometimes find myself pondering these answers. Often I receive a new revelation, see how I can correct something that hasn't gone well, or change my mind on something that is important to me.

If you would like to learn more about meditation, I suggest you look up meditation or chakras on the Internet. You will be surprised by how widely the subject is discussed.

I wish you good luck and many new and valuable insights into your personality.

Other Books by Bruno Gideon

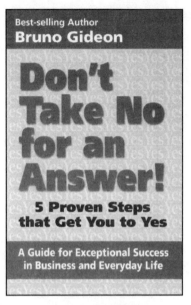

Matterhorn Publishing
$21.95 paperback, 216 pages
ISBN 0-9732491-1-0

"A great read for everyone. Bruno Gideon draws on his very considerable experience and amazing success in providing steps that really work!"

— Elaine Dembe, bestselling author of *Use the Good Dishes*

"This is an excellent book. I recommend it to everyone wishing to improve their negotiating skills and to get what they want without hurting others."

— Peter Urs Bender, bestselling author of *Leadership from Within*

"... exceptional ... as readable as it is constructive."

— David Cobain, *Financial Post*

"Tells you how to get your own way without banging your fist on the negotiating table."

— Dale Goldhawk, talk show host